New Directions for
Community Colleges

Arthur M. Cohen
EDITOR-IN-CHIEF

Richard L. Wagoner
ASSOCIATE EDITOR

Gabriel Jones
MANAGING EDITOR

P9-ARY-090

Advancing the Regional Role of Two-Year Colleges

L. Allen Phelps
EDITOR

Number 157 • Spring 2012
Jossey-Bass
San Francisco

ADVANCING THE REGIONAL ROLE OF TWO-YEAR COLLEGES
L. Allen Phelps (ed.)
New Directions for Community Colleges, no. 157

Arthur M. Cohen, Editor-in-Chief
Richard L. Wagoner, Associate Editor
Gabriel Jones, Managing Editor

NEW DIRECTIONS FOR COMMUNITY COLLEGES (ISSN 0194-3081, electronic ISSN 1536-0733) is part of The Jossey-Bass Higher and Adult Education Series and is published quarterly by Wiley Subscription Services, Inc., A Wiley Company, at Jossey-Bass, One Montgomery St., Ste. 1200, San Francisco, CA 94104. Periodicals Postage Paid at San Francisco, California, and at additional mailing offices. POSTMASTER: Send address changes to New Directions for Community Colleges, Jossey-Bass, One Montgomery St., Ste. 1200, San Francisco, CA 94104.

SUBSCRIPTIONS cost $89.00 for individuals and $275.00 for institutions, agencies, and libraries in the United States. Prices subject to change.

EDITORIAL CORRESPONDENCE should be sent to the Editor-in-Chief, Arthur M. Cohen, at the Graduate School of Education and Information Studies, University of California, Box 951521, Los Angeles, CA 90095-1521. All manuscripts receive anonymous reviews by external referees.

New Directions for Community Colleges is indexed in CIJE: Current Index to Journals in Education (ERIC), Contents Pages in Education (T&F), Current Abstracts (EBSCO), Ed/Net (Simpson Communications), Education Index/Abstracts (H. W. Wilson), Educational Research Abstracts Online (T&F), ERIC Database (Education Resources Information Center), and Resources in Education (ERIC).

Microfilm copies of issues and articles are available in 16mm and 35mm, as well as microfiche in 105mm, through University Microfilms Inc., 300 North Zeeb Road, Ann Arbor, MI 48106-1346.

CONTENTS

EDITOR'S NOTES

In the midst of a challenging economic recovery, the nation's policymakers and education leaders are seeking new and potentially more effective strategies to align personal and public educational investments with job creation, increased levels of employment, small business development, and entrepreneurial activity. Through their career and technical education programs and workforce training contracts, U.S. community colleges have historically played a prominent role in economic and workforce development. As Kasper noted in the Summer 2009 Special Issue of *NDCC*, the community college's curriculum sets it apart from other institutions of higher education by the many courses offered that enhance students' immediate career opportunities, especially with local employers. However, as recent commissioned studies have noted, the global economy, widespread use of information technology tools, and the lengthy recession have fundamentally changed the game. In two-year colleges, optimal solutions in the new economy will require leaders to think, design, and enact innovations regionally, but with close attention to global opportunities as well as local workforce needs and priorities.

In recent federal and state policy dialogues, community and technical colleges have been widely touted as strategic, transformative agents for innovation, which in turn can create solutions for an economic recovery and for sustaining rural communities. In the 2009 State of the Union, President Barack Obama set forth an ambitious agenda for U.S. postsecondary education by outlining a national college completion goal: *by 2020, to once again have the highest proportion of college graduates in the world.* Reaching this goal will require U.S. colleges to produce an estimated 8.2 million additional graduates, including 5 million additional graduates from two-year colleges.

Beginning in 2007–2008, the economic downturn heightened regional differences and outcome gaps in the United States. Depending on their location and residence, Americans have experienced minimal, moderate, or high rates of unemployment, plant closures, layoffs, declines in public services, and tax increases. These regional trends create particular and potentially unique challenges for two-year colleges and their leaders in addressing the national college completion goal. Recent data from the U.S. Bureau of Economic Analysis reflect growing disparities in regional contributions to U.S. growth over the past decade. In 2008, the national per-capita gross domestic product (GDP) grew a modest 0.7 percent to $37,899. In 2005, the Bureau of Economic Analysis reported the regional per-capita GDP

New Directions for Community Colleges, no. 157, Spring 2012 © 2012 Wiley Periodicals, Inc.
Published online in Wiley Online Library (wileyonlinelibrary.com) • DOI: 10.1002/cc.20001

output gap was $9,577, which reflected a 22 percent disparity between the highest and lowest regional GDP output. However, by 2008 the regional per-capita GDP output gap had risen to $11,894 or roughly 26 percent. In the five-state Great Lakes region (Michigan, Ohio, Wisconsin, Illinois, and Indiana), for example, the regional per-capita GDP for 2008 was $35,280, well below the national average of $37,899.

Reaching the 2020 national college completion goal will require some powerful and persistent innovations in two-year colleges, particularly in regions where economic challenges are more deeply entrenched. In states with healthier economies, (e.g., Minnesota, North Dakota, New York, and Connecticut), the Lumina Foundation predicts that considerably lower annual growth rates in postsecondary degree completion will be needed (3.1% to 4.7%) as compared to the Great Lakes region (5.4% to 6.4%). Within regions, two-year colleges are called on increasingly to collaborate in new ways with employers, universities, K through 12 schools, and governmental agencies in regional approaches to create new forms of economic, social, and human capital.

Grounded in the Midwestern context, this Special Issue examines several promising policies and innovations that re-envision the role of two-year colleges in developing regional rather than local solutions to the emerging economic and educational challenges. Many of the chapters, which emanated from a recent colloquium on Re-visioning Two-Year Colleges in the Midwest, held at the University of Wisconsin–Madison, examine regional approaches for addressing priorities such as raising literacy levels, improving the skills of displaced workers, aligning education and career pathways, and supporting the adoption of new technologies in the workplace. Overall, the volume addresses two signature questions:

1. What key themes are embedded in regionally focused, two-year college innovations and policy priorities?
2. What strategies can be used to expand the regional capacity for innovation, leadership, and research in the two-year college sector?

While many of the authors describe Midwestern regional innovations, each chapter concludes with recommendations for college leaders without regard to the regional particulars.

In Chapter One, I examine the challenges of and opportunities for enhancing regional higher education collaboration with particular attention to expanding the regional role for two-year colleges. Following a discussion of why and how regional approaches matter in enhancing economic impact and improving educational quality, eight signature themes and a set of action strategies are outlined for expanding regional approaches to improving postsecondary education.

Chapters Two and Three offer some valuable insights on the future of Midwestern community and technical colleges. Authored by John Austin of the Brookings Institution, Chapter Two describes a regional growth strategy, one featuring enhanced collaboration between two-year colleges and research universities. In Chapter Three, Jeff Rafn provides a rich case study of regional collaboration spanning the past decade, involving ten two-year colleges, three four-year universities, and, more recently, a new regional economic development partnership.

Chapters Four through Eight offer detailed analyses of policies and practices emblematic of the regional collaboration themes identified in papers from a recent Midwestern colloquium on Re-visioning Two-Year Colleges in the Midwest. While the chapters feature community college innovations in the eight-state Midwest region, the authors offer recommendations for community college leaders regardless of regional contexts.

In Chapter Four, Janet Washbon describes several key features of Wisconsin's technical colleges that enable the colleges to address the rapid technological changes occurring in manufacturing, health care, information technology, and other sectors. Increasingly, programs and learning opportunities are situated in settings that meet the needs of both employers and students.

Debra Bragg, Laura Dresser, and Whitney Smith describe the Joyce Foundation's Shifting Gears initiative in Chapter Five. Working in selected Illinois and Wisconsin two-year colleges over the past five years, this initiative has created and demonstrated the value of career pathway and bridge programs for educated low-skilled workers needing both developmental and technical education.

Chapter Six, authored by Jason Tyszko and Robert Sheets, describes the Illinois Talent Development Project. Designed to provide student teams with authentic and discovery-focused project-based learning experiences identified by industry partners, the implications for using this instructional approach in two-year colleges are discussed.

In Chapter Seven, Todd Lundberg offers persuasive evidence for shifting the role of general education in two-year colleges to focus on twenty-first-century problem solving and inquiry skills. Such skills, he argues, are a vital aspect of the innovation talent needed in business and community settings.

Echoing the challenges outlined in Chapter Two by Austin, Allen Phelps and Amy Prevost document in Chapter Eight various community college efforts to promote student research experiences and to strengthen faculty involvement in research partnerships.

In Chapter Nine, Christopher Matheny and Clifton Conrad offer a framework to guide the decisions of two-year college leaders when they are advancing regional innovations and initiatives.

As noted earlier, the chapters presented herein emanated from a recent colloquium sponsored by the School of Education at UW–Madison. Dean Julie Underwood and members of the planning team provided valuable insights for framing the agenda and topics addressed at the colloquium:

Clifton Conrad, Sara Goldrick-Rab, Gregory Lampe, Noel Radomski, Christopher Rasmussen, Janet Washbon, and John Wiley. Martha Kantor, U.S. Deputy Secretary of Education, offered provocative opening-session remarks encouraging the eighty-five invited participants to think and act boldly in creating regionally focused community college policies, innovations, and partnerships. Gail Kiles Krumenauer managed the colloquium project with timely, cogent, and supportive facilitate.

Finally, this volume is dedicated to Morgan, Olivia, Matthew, Hunter, and Lincoln, my spectacular grandchildren, whose future well being will be anchored, I trust, in the student-centered college learning environments and experiences described herein.

L. Allen Phelps
Editor

L. ALLEN PHELPS is a professor emeritus of Educational Leadership and Policy Analysis and former director of the Center on Education and Work at the University of Wisconsin–Madison.

NEW DIRECTIONS FOR COMMUNITY COLLEGES • DOI: 10.1002/cc

This opening chapter describes why regional approaches to postsecondary education policy and implementation matter in the current economic and social context. Eight signature themes and strategies for regional two-year college innovation are introduced.

1

Regionalizing Postsecondary Education for the Twenty-First Century: Promising Innovations and Capacity Challenges

L. Allen Phelps

Without question, U.S. postsecondary institutions are facing monumental challenges in meeting the rapidly evolving demands for preparing a well-educated twenty-first-century citizenry. As the changing landscape of higher and postsecondary education is increasingly linked to and driven by economic recovery, the role of two-year colleges is changing dramatically. Over the past twenty years, rapid globalization and the intensive use of information technology in all sectors of society have changed the formula for preparing the nation's workforce. The boundaries of our economy are no longer defined primarily by city, county, or state borders. Rather, the formula and strategies for preparing workers and communities for the twenty-first century must include and capitalize on regional economic interests—that is, interests defined by a diverse group of industries needing key assets such as infrastructure support, investment, and the availability of local talent.

In launching the Workforce Innovation in Regional Economic Development (WIRED) initiative in 2006, the U.S. Department of Labor noted that the economic reality of global competition has created emerging regional opportunity contexts in which

> companies, workers, researchers, entrepreneurs and governments come together to create a competitive advantage. That advantage stems from the

New Directions for Community Colleges, no. 157, Spring 2012 © 2012 Wiley Periodicals, Inc.
Published online in Wiley Online Library (wileyonlinelibrary.com) • DOI: 10.1002/cc.20002

ability to transform new ideas and new knowledge into advanced, high quality products or services—in other words, to innovate. And those regions that are successful demonstrate the ability to network innovation assets—people, institutions, capital and infrastructure—to generate growth and prosperity in the region's economy.

Concurrently, the emergence of regional innovation economies creates and strengthens regional partnerships among key players, including schools, community colleges, universities, adult education providers, regional employers, and economic and workforce development organizations.

In recent federal and state policy dialogues, community and technical colleges have been widely touted as strategic transformative agents for innovation and as new solutions in economic recovery and sustaining rural communities. In his 2009 State of the Union address, President Barack Obama set forth an ambitious agenda for U.S. postsecondary education by outlining a national college completion goal: by 2020, to once again have the highest proportion of college graduates in the world. Reaching this goal will require U.S. colleges to produce an estimated 8.2 million additional graduates, including 5 million additional graduates from two-year colleges.

In this opening chapter, separate sections examine the anchoring ingredients of the regional strategies through which two-year colleges are responding to local, regional, and in some cases broader needs deemed critical to generating and sustaining economic productivity and other forms of social and civic capital. First, drawing on recent European literature, I examine why regional agendas for postsecondary education policy and implementation are being considered in the United States and abroad. Second, the chapter provides an overview of the regional context and challenges confronting Midwestern two-year colleges, as they address the president's college completion goals and other societal priorities. Finally, I briefly describe eight signature regional innovation strategies generated by a recent Midwestern colloquium on the topic. The subsequent Special Issue chapters describe several Midwestern two-year college innovations conducted by state agencies, foundations, and regional networks of colleges committed to changing the outcomes for students, colleges, and the regional economy.

Why Regions Matter

In the post-economic crisis, policymakers, business leaders, educators, and citizens in the United States and abroad share a common goal: to stimulate new and sustainable growth. A team of geographers and economists at the Organization for Economic Cooperation and Development in Paris have studied long-term regional economic growth data across thirty nations

(OECD, 2009); by developing multiple econometric models from large data sets in multiple countries, they are able to predict the optimal economic growth factors guiding higher-functioning economies. Some of the OECD's education-relevant findings include:

1. Human capital and innovation positively influence regional growth.
2. Infrastructure (e.g., educational institutions, investment) is a necessary but not sufficient condition for growth; human capital and innovation must be present.
3. Investments in infrastructure and human capital require three years to positively influence growth.
4. Educational attainment is a key enabling factor. Public investment in infrastructure has a positive effect on regional growth. However, the effect is much stronger when educational attainment is high. Additionally, there is a strong positive relationship between tertiary education (college degrees) and economic growth measured by patenting activity.
5. While leading regions are important for national economies, in the past decade lagging regions have made a strong contribution to growth. In most of the OECD countries studied, they have generated more than 50 percent of the national growth in the past decade.

Overall, the OECD regional growth policy analysis suggests that more attention to lagging regions can be helpful for addressing growing social challenges and inequities (e.g., poverty and educational attainment) and improving economic performance (e.g., increasing GDP). The authors argue that regional policies should make a strong and explicit link between these outcomes.

Since 2007–2008 the economic downturn has created or heightened notable differences across regions of the United States. Depending on their location and residence, Americans have experienced minimal, moderate, or high rates of unemployment, plant closures, layoffs and furloughs, declines in public services, and tax increases. The rapidly changing economic landscape has challenged community colleges to generate responsive programs that address three regionally nuanced hard realities: (1) the nation is experiencing a significant loss of traditional well-paying jobs, (2) the good jobs available for younger workers require additional postsecondary education levels such as bachelor's degrees for entry-level work in many fields, and (3) for both incumbent and dislocated workers, acquiring and continuously updating occupational skills is an individual responsibility. Most of today's employers provide only minimal education and training opportunities (Jacobs, 2011). The regional industry sector concentration pattern of technical skills and expertise often has a profound influence in shaping the economic development and human talent development roles of two-year colleges (see Chapters 2 and 3).

These regional patterns create particular and potentially unique challenges for two-year colleges and their leaders in addressing the national college completion goal. Recent data from the U.S. Bureau of Economic Analysis (Coakley, Reed, and Taylor, 2009) reflect growing disparities in regional contributions to U.S. growth over the past decade. In 2008, the national per-capita gross domestic product (GDP) grew a modest 0.7 percent to $37,899. Only three of the eight U.S. multistate regions had per-capita GDP output at or above the national average. In 2005, the Bureau of Economic Analysis reported the regional per-capita GDP output gap was $9,577, which reflected a 22 percent disparity between the highest and lowest regional GDP output. However, by 2008, the regional per-capita GDP output gap had risen to $11,894, or roughly 26 percent. In the five-state Great Lakes region (Michigan, Ohio, Wisconsin, Illinois, and Indiana), for example, the regional per-capita GDP for 2008 was $35,280, well below the national average of $37,899.

Reaching the 2020 national college completion goal will require some powerful two-year college innovations, particularly in states or regions where economic challenges are more deeply entrenched. In states with healthier economies (e.g., Minnesota, North Dakota, New York, and Connecticut), the Lumina Foundation (2011) predicts that considerably lower annual growth rates in postsecondary degree completion will be needed (3.1 to 4.7 percent). In the lagging Great Lakes Region, where recent unemployment rates are higher and the 2008 per-capita GDP output was only 78 percent of the highest-performing economic region in the United States, the annual postsecondary degree completion rates will have to improve by 5.4 to 6.4 percent across the five states. Within regions, two-year colleges are called upon increasingly to collaborate in new ways with employers, universities, K through 12 schools, and governmental agencies in regional approaches to create new forms of economic, social, and human capital.

Why the Midwest Region Matters

In America's Midwest, the economic downturn has created a heightened interest in postsecondary education responses and solutions for addressing the uncertainties ahead. The economic challenges arising over the past two decades in the Midwest are well chronicled. As Richard Longworth, author of *Caught in the Middle: America's Heartland in the Age of Globalism*, concludes, "The first era of Midwestern history is over. The next one has begun. We can make of it what we will" (2008, p. 267). Important lessons and valuable policy insights can be gleaned from the past, as well as from the evolving responses for rebuilding the Midwest. As a recent issue of *Time* magazine suggests, Detroit is a window into the challenges facing all of America, and serves as a bellwether for benchmarking progress: "From urban planning to the crisis of manufacturing, from the lingering role of race and class in our society to the struggle for better health care and education, it's all happening at its most extreme in the Motor City" (Huey, 2009, p. 4).

Over the past century, Midwestern cities and farming communities have had a profound influence on the growth of manufacturing and agricultural productivity technologies. The expansion of the automotive and agricultural sectors created economic opportunities for millions of immigrants and Americans who relocated to the Midwest for high-paying jobs. Large Midwestern cities such as Detroit, Cleveland, Chicago, and Milwaukee gave birth to the industrial era and the nation's middle class. The Midwestern education system was created by and for an industrial era that must now be re-imagined for the digital, multicultural global economy. Without question, new visions and learning agendas are vital ingredients in the calculus for the integrated human-economic-social capital that can sustain the small towns and urban centers of the nation's heartland. The community and technical colleges with their comprehensive missions and capacity to partner with K-through-12 schools, universities, communities, businesses, nonprofit organizations, and governments can play an integral synergistic role in creating the next generation of the Midwestern economic and cultural landscape.

Grounded in the Midwestern context, this Special Issue examines several promising policies and innovations that recast the role of two-year colleges in developing regional rather than local solution strategies for key missions, including raising literacy levels, improving the skills of displaced workers, aligning education and career pathways, and supporting the adoption of new technologies in the workplace. Using both regional and national perspectives, the chapters examine multiple challenges and opportunities for advancing regional missions and agendas for two-year colleges. Overall, the volume addresses two guiding questions: (1) What key themes are embedded in regionally focused two-year college innovations and policy priorities?, and (2) What strategies can be used to expand the regional capacity for innovation, leadership, and research in the two-year college sector?

Two-year community and technical colleges, a uniquely American institution, were invented more than a century ago by Midwestern school and university leaders who saw the importance of local post–high school graduation programs for young adults and the emerging era of agricultural mechanization. Opening in 1901, Joliet Junior College was the nation's first public community college and helped fuel the rise of the manufacturing economy. After more than a century of unprecedented yet relatively unrecognized growth, Midwestern community and technical colleges are deeply respected for their commitment to creating full and equitable educational opportunities for a wide spectrum of learners, making college learning affordable and accessible, strengthening the economy, and enhancing the quality of life for all citizens.

NEW DIRECTIONS FOR COMMUNITY COLLEGES • DOI: 10.1002/cc

Times are changing, however. Across the Midwest and throughout the nation, the importance and urgency for education reform has never been higher or more intensely conveyed. Framed by new imperatives, our national policy is now one that inextricably links educational attainment to economic prosperity and security:

> In a global economy where the most valuable skill you can sell is your knowledge, a good education is no longer just a pathway to opportunity—it is a pre-requisite. The countries that out-teach us today will out-compete us tomorrow. [President Barack Obama, 2/24/09]

Beyond positing challenging benchmarks, the White House has mapped a series of key themes for strategies to align educational access with the development of expanded workforce and economic growth capacities. Themes include preparing dislocated workers for local or regional high-skill and high-wage employment opportunities, using robust evidence to design programs, and tracking student success in college, during transfer, and in the workplace. In announcing the American Graduation Initiative (AGI) in July 2009 at Macomb Community College in a Detroit suburb, the president asserted clearly:

> Now is the time to build a firmer, stronger foundation for growth that will not only withstand future economic storms, but one that helps us thrive and compete in a global economy. It's time to reform our community colleges so that they provide Americans of all ages a chance to learn the skills and knowledge necessary to compete for the jobs of the future.

Additionally, a number of foundations, state governments, and national and regional public policy organizations have made major commitments to strengthening Midwestern postsecondary education. These emerging two-year college investment priorities focus on a plethora of key issues, including but not limited to expanding the capacity of two-year colleges to more effectively serve low-income students, first-generation students, and students of color as well as adult workers, and responding effectively to skills and workforce development needs of extant and emerging research-driven economic sectors, including health care, the automotive industry, energy renewal, and bio-fuels. In 2007, the Joyce Foundation launched the Shifting Gears initiative in six states—Illinois, Indiana, Michigan, Minnesota, Ohio, and Wisconsin—to redesign and align adult education, workforce development, and postsecondary education policies to support economic growth and expand job opportunities for low-skilled workers in the Midwest (Joyce Foundation, 2011). The catalytic role of two-year colleges in these initiatives is described in Chapter 5. The Midwest Digital Fabrication Partnership (MDFP) is a three-year National Science Foundation (NSF) investment in two community colleges and one university. The MDFP is integrating Massachusetts Institute of Technology (MIT)-based digital fabrication capabilities and resources into student-learning experiences at the undergraduate levels of higher education. The major goals of the project are to (1) integrate digital fabrication laboratories into selected product realization courses to provide enhanced hands-on science, technology, engineering, and mathematics (STEM) learning experiences; (2) assess the ability of digital fabrication laboratory experiences to enhance student STEM competencies and attitudes; and (3) evaluate digital fabrication laboratories as a STEM recruitment vehicle. The infrastructure and disruptive innovation strategies used by the MDFP and other NSF regional networks are examples of the partnerships described in Chapter 8.

Several Midwestern states are active partners in the Achieving the Dream (ATD): Community Colleges Count network. This national nonprofit organization helps community college students succeed, particularly students of color and low-income students. The organization works on multiple fronts, including efforts on campuses and in research, public engagement, and public policy. In the five states of the Great Lakes region, twenty-nine community colleges are active ATD participants and are undertaking a number of data analysis, professional development, and program alignment innovations to improve the success of low-income students and students of color.

As these three examples illustrate, the Midwest is prepared to reinvest in transforming community and technical colleges; the regional capacity for creating and supporting innovation and strengthening leadership will be pivotal to the success of these investments.

Regional Innovation and Leadership: Signature Themes and Strategies

With collaborative support from the Midwestern Higher Education Compact, the University of Wisconsin Colleges, and the Wisconsin Technical College System, a team of faculty members at the University of Wisconsin–Madison convened a two-day colloquium in summer 2009. The goal of the colloquium was twofold: (1) to describe promising Midwestern two-year college innovations and (2) to begin mapping the research and leadership capacities needed to scale-up promising innovations. During the two-day forum nearly eighty invited Midwestern leaders representing the technical college; community college; university, state, and federal government; and policymaking sectors reviewed a series of academic papers and presentations describing and documenting promising innovations and emerging policy proposals. To capture participants' insights and priorities, the latter portion of the colloquium agenda featured facilitated dialogue sessions, which generated group responses to the guiding questions.

Regionalizing Postsecondary Education: Signature Themes and Strategies.   A detailed content analysis of the papers and presentation materials presented at the Colloquium revealed eight signature themes. The chapters that follow elaborate on and explore the challenges associated with the implementation of the themes.

NEW DIRECTIONS FOR COMMUNITY COLLEGES • DOI: 10.1002/cc

1. *Thinking and working regionally with both a local and a global perspective*
   - Reanimate the Midwest's role as educator for the world by creating a globally recognized regional identity—one that serves as a market-place magnet and provides students and businesses with a value-added competitive advantage. (Austin, Chapter 2)
   - Generate regional education visions and strategies that include (a) providing quality seamless education and essential educational resources for communities, businesses, and government, and (b) driving regional economic vitality. (Rafn, Chapter 3)
   - Fuel the power of the free-agent human-capital marketplace with flexible, portable credentials (e.g., a regional, in-state tuition compact). (Austin, Chapter 2)
2. *Broadening access and ensuring success for diverse students*
   - Reengineering adult education, workforce development, and postsecondary education policies is an essential strategy to support economic growth and expand job opportunities for low-skilled workers in the Midwestern economy. (Bragg, Dresser, and Smith, Chapter 5)
   - Create modularized, flexible instruction focused on basic and college readiness skills to serve the significant population of low-income students with less than a high school diploma who are pursuing two-year college programs. (Bragg, Dresser, and Smith, Chapter 5)
   - Generate strategies for alignment of readiness skills with college credit in programs that secure positions on a career ladder in a sustainable employment sector. (Bragg, Dresser, and Smith, Chapter 5)
3. *Engaging K-through-20 learning and teaching with a search for authentic, real-world solutions to major societal and cultural problems*
   - Think about teaching and learning as an innovation talent development process; one characterized by teams of learners consulting with business and community groups to generate solutions to authentic challenges could be a centerpiece for college transformation initiatives. (Tyzsko and Sheets, Chapter 6; Lundberg, Chapter 7)
4. *Strengthening instruction and assessment*
   - Aligning assessment evidence with both developmental–noncredit instruction and college credit instruction pushes the envelope of conventional thinking in productive ways among community college stakeholders. (Bragg, Dresser, and Smith, Chapter 5)
   - Using real-world technology tools and platforms to design, deliver, and assess learning can provide an interface with common-core learning standards as well as instructional and information technology standards. (Tyzsko and Sheets, Chapter 6; Lundberg, Chapter 7)
5. *Leveraging value-added research and transfer education partnerships with four-year institutions*
   - With research universities emerging as economic engines, two-year colleges will assume a significantly larger and different role in the higher and postsecondary education landscape. (Austin, Chapter 2)

- Creating partnerships between technical colleges and four-year universities has yielded new *earning-focused, value-added community assets* such as dental clinics for low-income families. In these partnerships, researchers and faculty members from both settings have access to authentic real-world circumstances in which their research and teaching have multiple payoffs for communities, students, and research programs. (Washbon, Chapter 4; Lundberg, Chapter 7)
- Develop and expand research investments by the National Science Foundation and other foundations to support joint research opportunities between four-year and two-year college faculty. (Phelps and Prevost, Chapter 8)
- Exploiting research opportunities for community college students in research labs can optimize undergraduate learning. (Phelps and Prevost, Chapter 8)

6. *Aligning talent development pathways*
    - Exploiting regional partnerships among high schools, postsecondary institutions, and employers will create human resource development pathways, such as the Fox Valley Engineering Pipeline, for place-bound students. (Bragg, Dresser, and Smith, Chapter 5)
    - Advancing efforts to build talent development pathways should be aligned with the national efforts of state leaders to structure industry-supported, locally viable career clusters and pathways.

7. *Leading successful change and innovation*
    - Strengthening the leadership of administrators to address stability and change in turbulent times entails explicit attention to the learning needs of leaders and their communities. (Rafn, Chapter 3)
    - Framing and using systemic concepts enables management of the complex relationships between the organization and its larger societal context, including schools, business, and governmental and community agencies. (Rafn, Chapter 3)
    - Sustaining cooperation and interorganizational collaboration among multiple stakeholders depends on mutually beneficial exchanges based on enlightened self-interest and characterized by trust, shared goals, complementary contributions, and equitable benefits. (Rafn, Chapter 3)
    - Leading successful change and innovation efforts in two-year college settings is fundamentally central to fulfilling missions, visions, and performance expectations and standards. (Matheny and Conrad, Chapter 9)
    - Considering academic change in the culture of two-year colleges requires leaders to be proficient in managing change in response to internal and external sources that require a balanced focus on institutional and regional quality or impact. (Matheny and Conrad, Chapter 9)

8. *Building evidence-based cultures and systems*
  - Creating and building consensus for measurable national and institutional performance goals must guide the re-visioning of two-year institutions. (Rafn, Chapter 3; Bragg, Dresser, and Smith, Chapter 5)
  - Improving the use of student-level data systems in two-year college settings is vital to documenting and learning about the success of students, faculty, programs, and institutional partnerships. (Bragg, Dresser, and Smith, Chapter 5)
  - Supplementing national or state trends with well-designed employer surveys, industry-based advisory committees, and targeted focus group discussions with the college's employer community can provide more accurate and useful sources of information about regional demand in new and emerging occupations, changes in the content of established occupations, and the need to modify or even eliminate current programs. (Washbon, Chapter 4)
  - Documenting the impact of two-year colleges must include new metrics and measures for the learning-based, valued-added community assets that are created and delivered by such entities as small-business incubators, dental clinics for low-income families, or countywide emergency operations centers that serve as backups for county governments. (Washbon, Chapter 4)

Summary Implications

While these themes and strategies for regional community college innovation partnerships are grounded in the Midwestern context, the same economic, social, human capital dynamics are at work in other U.S. regions. From 2005 to 2007, the U.S. Department of Labor funded thirty-nine regional WIRED (Workforce Innovation Regional Economic Development) initiatives, including twenty-nine that operate outside the Midwest. Each of these regions received between $5 million and $15 million over three years to implement and demonstrate "the critical role talent development plays in creating effective regional economic development strategies" (U.S. Department of Labor, 2006). A recent third-party evaluation of the WIRED initiative indicates that community colleges were often extensively involved with industry and Workforce Investment Boards in prior planning of regional workforce development efforts, as well as a prominent, highly involved partner in the second- and third-generation WIRED grants (Hewat and Hollenbeck, 2009). This evidence suggests that two-year colleges, regardless of their regional location, are a prominent actor and stakeholder in the new global economy.

Beyond the Department of Labor's WIRED Initiative, several nationally prominent economic and educational challenges require local two-year college leaders everywhere to proactively seek out regional partners for a variety of strategic priorities:

1. The decline in state and federal funding for community colleges suggests clearly that options for regional cost-savings be considered. Chief among the options are: joint faculty development activities, interinstitutional teaching appointments, regional sharing of instructional facilities, and other efficiency-gaining measures described in the chapters that follow. As always, it is important to ensure that regional efficiency measures do not limit or reduce the quality of instruction or student and institutional outcomes.

2. Because two-year colleges serve nearly half of all undergraduates, including many from underrepresented backgrounds and low-income and first-generation families, student access and success is an imperative. Among other college access strategies, regional tuition reciprocity policies can serve many purposes: build enrollment to strengthen programs, improve efficiency by filing excess capacity, and enhance student diversity. Further, for two-year colleges bordering other states or regions, tuition reciprocity allows the citizens of nearby communities to be served conveniently. Strategies for improving student success can be enhanced through a number of regional partnership efforts, including the career pathway and bridge programs for developmental and low-skilled learners described in Chapter 5.

3. Expanded regional partnerships can provide resources and options to address the shifting missions of community colleges, and perhaps more importantly, the outcome expectations of a rapidly growing, increasingly diverse population of students.

References

Coakley, C. A., Reed, D. A., and Taylor, S. L. "Gross Domestic Product by State." *Survey of Current Business*, June 2009. Retrieved November 9, 2010, from http://www.bea.gov/scb/pdf/2009/06%20June/0609_gdp_state.pdf

Hewat, N., and Hollenbeck, K. "Nurturing America's Growth in the Global Marketplace through Talent Development: An Interim Report on the Evaluation of Generations II and III of WIRED." 2009. Report submitted to the U.S. Department of Labor, Employment and Training Administration.

Huey, J. "Assignment Detroit." *Time*, October 5, 2009, 4, 174.

Jacobs, J. "Hard Lessons Learned from the Economic Recession." *Community College Times*, February 2, 2011. Retrieved March 28, 2011, from http://www.communitycollegetimes.com/Pages/Workforce-Development/Hard-lessons-learned-from-the-recession.aspx

Joyce Foundation (2011). "Shifting Gears" Retrieved October 14, 2011, from http://www.joycefdn.org/content.cfm/shifting-gears

Longworth, R. C. *Caught in the Middle: America's Heartland in the Age of Globalism*. New York: Bloomsbury, 2008.

Lumina Foundation. "Education Attainment Levels for the States." 2011. Retrieved February 10, 2011, from http://www.luminafoundation.org/state_data/

Obama, B. "Remarks of President Barack Obama—State of the Union." Delivered to Joint Session of Congress, February 24, 2009, para. 66

Obama, B. "Remarks at Macomb Community College in Warren, Michigan, July 14, 2009." Retrieved December 17, 2009, from http://www.gpoaccess.gov/presdocs/2009/DCPD-200900565.pdf

Organization for Economic Co-operation and Development (OECD). *Regions Matter: Economic Recovery, Innovation and Sustainable Growth.* Paris: Organization for Economic Co-operation and Development, 2009.

U.S. Department of Labor. *Workforce Innovation in Regional Economic Development.* Washington, D.C.: Employment and Training Administration, February 2006, p. 1. Retrieved March 28, 2011, from http://www.doleta.gov/wired/files/WIRED_overview.pdf

L. ALLEN PHELPS *is a professor emeritus of Educational Leadership and Policy Analysis and former director of the Center on Education and Work at the University of Wisconsin–Madison.*

NEW DIRECTIONS FOR COMMUNITY COLLEGES • DOI: 10.1002/cc

2

The Midwest led the creation of the modern community college and public university, designed to support the advance of the industrial economy that grew to be centered in the region. In today's knowledge-driven economy the role of learning and research institutions has changed dramatically. Looking forward, these institutions must change and contribute in new ways to the region's economic prosperity.

Reanimating the Vital Center: Challenges and Opportunities in the Regional Talent Development Pipeline

John Austin

Introduction

The mighty heartland of the United States, the American Midwest, is certainly struggling economically. This region was the epicenter of America's industrial revolution, the arsenal of democracy in World War II, and the builder of the great blue-collar middle class that personified the American Dream. This important region made America a global agricultural and industrial powerhouse. The recent collapse of the auto industry, one of its signature industries embodies the transformational challenge the region faces—from literal invention and dominance of the mass-production factory economy to finding its place, products, and wealth-earning potential in a new global knowledge economy.

Learning and research institutions, including two-year colleges, have played a huge role in the region's economic development. They can also play the signature role in its future, but in new ways. The biggest challenge and opportunity is to take the expansive learning infrastructure built largely to serve the twentieth century agro-industrial economy and repurpose it to serve the emerging knowledge economy. Moreover, we must capitalize on it as a regional identifier, a magnet, and a source of comparative advantage.

NEW DIRECTIONS FOR COMMUNITY COLLEGES, no. 157, Spring 2012 © 2012 Wiley Periodicals, Inc.
Published online in Wiley Online Library (wileyonlinelibrary.com) • DOI: 10.1002/cc.20003

Economic Context

In 2006, the Brookings Institution published "The Vital Center" (Austin and Affolter-Caine), a report on the history, size, scope, and unique economic strengths and challenges of an overlapping twelve-state agro-industrial economic region, encompassing the Great Lakes and the upper Mississippi and Ohio river watersheds. This is a region that is highly integrated economically, but, even more significantly, shares a similar economic and social position and arc of development today.

In 2007, acknowledging and documenting the common economic development history and highly interdependent economies of the bi-national Great Lakes region, B. Affolter-Caine and I enhanced and extended this analysis to incorporate Canada through a follow-up work, "The Vital Connection."

In 2010, Brookings then released a follow-up paper, "The Next Economy: Economic Recovery and Transformation in the Great Lakes Region," which notes the unique role the region's community colleges and universities play in the period of global recession, as well as the regional economic adaptation to structural change in dominant industries, most notably the U.S. auto industry.

Working independently, former journalist and Chicago Council on Global Affairs senior fellow Richard Longworth provided insightful reporting and detail to the uneven and uncertain adaptation of the American heartland in his book, *Caught in the Middle: America's Heartland in the Age of Globalism* (2008). This work focused on a similar geography, an eight-state region stretching from Ohio to Iowa, with shared economic challenges brought on by globalization.

Longworth sees globalization as a potentially affirmative force, but one that is testing the Midwest's productivity and resilience. Storied cities such as St. Louis, Cleveland, and Detroit are struggling to keep pace with their counterparts in the race to access globalization's benefits. Some of the Midwest is beginning the economic restructuring and diversification from its industrial past, but the region's economic growth continues to lag behind the rest of the United States. He suggests that cities and states spend too much time and money holding onto old industries and too little on the needs of the future, including education. Many old factory towns and cities wonder if they have a future at all.

All these analyses point to the unique challenges the Midwest faces, given its particular economic and social development pattern. These challenges are directly informed by the region's role as the engine of the agro-industrial economy. This is the region where the move from farm to factory, from fieldwork to cities with their great industrial combines, occurred on the grandest scale, and bore the greatest fruit in terms of job and wealth creation. One need only mention the iconic names of the industrial barons who created the world's first vertically integrated corporations and located them in the Midwest: Rockefeller, Vanderbilt, Heinz, Ford, Carnegie, Pillsbury, Kellogg and Dow.

NEW DIRECTIONS FOR COMMUNITY COLLEGES • DOI: 10.1002/cc

On the challenge side of the equation this legacy of factory economy leadership leaves the region with big deficits in the currency of what matters in today's global knowledge economy:

- An employment culture, and by extension community culture, that came to rely on large paternal organizations and institutions to provide employment, benefits, and community stability
- Significantly diminished entrepreneurial activity and culture
- Comparatively low levels of educational attainment as so many individuals, families, and communities achieved middle-class status without higher education
- A battered and polluted landscape with "brownfields"; polluted rivers, streams, and harbors; and an aging infrastructure that practically screams "Rust Belt"
- Massive migration of black and multiethnic populations into these areas, coupled with white flight from cities, which led to intensely segregated communities
- Reliance on manufacturing jobs under global stress, giving rise to protectionist and xenophobic fears and sentiments
- Crumbling and segregated communities and the lack of perceived new opportunities, contributing to a talent flight and youthful brain drain
- A social compact built for the industrial and paternal era, when large employers financed retirement and health-care benefits and job losses were treated as a cyclical rather than a structural challenge, leaving workers and employers reeling and lacking support for transition to new jobs and skills

The irony is that these challenges, the legacies of factory-economy dominance, mask relevant assets that exist in the region and were developed concurrently to fuel the initial agro-industrial development. Among these attributes are:

- A natural infrastructure—one that, if cleaned and fixed up, would make the region a potentially very attractive locale for people to live, work, and do business in. The farms, forests, and rivers; the historic and interesting architecture of the older cities; and the unrivaled natural features of the Great Lakes and inland lakes all provide amenities and unique attributes to define the place as a choice location in today's increasingly mobile talent-driven economy.
- A global player in the economy. The region is still a huge marketplace and a global economic mega-region. It has active and connected firms, universities, and trade and commerce, and a vibrant exchange of ideas, as well as existing infrastructure for global connectivity.
- The innovation infrastructure that exists in the region—the research and learning institutions that were purposefully built in the region and that

exist on a scale and with horsepower truly unmatched on the globe. The opportunity is real to leverage this infrastructure as a primary fuel force for economic advance, given that the emerging knowledge economy means innovation is the coin of the economic realm, when new ideas, technologies, and talent are literally driving economic prosperity.

Industrial historian Peter Drucker, who first coined the term *knowledge worker* in his seminal 1959 text, *Landmarks of Tomorrow*, noted in 1994 in *The Age of Social Transformation* the critical importance of education and schooling. Drucker argues that knowledge has become the key resource, one that is fundamentally different from the traditional key resources noted by economists (land, labor, and capital), making the school and learning processes the center of society.

The Midwest region has more productive research and learning institutions than any place on earth—more public universities, more land-grant universities, and a more expansive network of community colleges. Clearly, this region has the opportunity to be the innovation center and the talent agglomeration center of the world. Considering the context of what they need to do today, I argue that the role of learning and research institutions has changed. Looking forward, they must contribute to economy prosperity.

Education and the Rise of Midwestern Agro-Industrial Might

Education was front and center in this region's economic and social development. The Northwest Ordinance, which laid out the region's political geography, gave us free labor, lots of local government, and education. Article III of the Ordinance begins: "Religion, morality, and knowledge being necessary to good government and the happiness of mankind, schools and the means of education shall forever be encouraged."

Under the Northwest Ordinance there was room reserved for a school in every township. Later, the land-grant and great regional public universities were created to provide high-quality, low-cost education to every man and woman, not just the elites, and to fuel commercial, industrial, and agricultural development.

Despite this regional head start toward education, however, higher education remained the province of the relative few. By the late 1940s, fewer than 10 percent of Americans had completed a college education. The community college movement built up considerable momentum after World War II, with the Midwest taking leadership in developing comprehensive institutions largely designed to extend the benefits of higher education to the emergent blue-collar and middle-class workforce.

The role of these educational institutions generally was a response to the needs and opportunities provided by the emergent agro-industrial economy: promoting the technical advance of agriculture and industry, preparing the managers as well as the technically trained and vocationally prepared cadres of industrial workers, and providing a baseline of literacy for all. As an example, the comprehensive high school, an innovation itself a century ago, was designed explicitly to serve this industrial economy. It essentially segmented learners into three tiers: the college-bound, those destined by genes or disposition for the technical and managerial roles in society; the vocational, those who worked with their hands on the farms and in the factories; and those who were merely socialized and provided with basic literacy.

Similarly, the postsecondary learning institutions so richly developed in the region were in large measure about producing inputs for the great blue-collar machinery—to develop the various role-players needed by the agro-industrial economy. Our great land-grant and public universities led the way in preparing applied researchers for new advances in farm and industrial technology as well as a managerial class of white-collar professionals to run the organizations and offices of farm, factory, commercial, and civic life (managers, accountants, salesmen, marketers, and doctors, along with the next generations of educators). Midwestern community colleges grew to better prepare the large cadre of vocationally trained professionals to play niche roles: electrician, skilled tradesman, assembler, repairman, truck driver, and other trade positions vital to the industrial economy.

As Macomb Community College president and leading community college scholar James Jacobs noted in his recent presidential inaugural remarks (2010): "While the first junior colleges were founded more than a century ago, the modern comprehensive community college is a phenomenon of the great post–World War II American expansion" with its center in the Midwest. Overall, 75 percent of today's community colleges were established between 1945 and 1975. These new institutions pioneered the concept of the comprehensive community college. Supported by the GI Bill, community college leaders believed a high school degree was not sufficient for acquiring the new technical skills needed by employers. They viewed community colleges as the providers of skills for middle-level occupations.

Jacobs also suggested that Midwestern community colleges pioneered the "comprehensive community college concept"—large multimission institutions whose main objective was to bring education to workers. While preparing workforces with the technical skills needed by the industrial economy, these colleges also extended to all working-age adults parts of the high school institution's functionality: socialization and basic literacy, along with vocational preparation and workforce development for niche roles, including increasingly customized training for industry. As a result, In the 1960s, many of the nation's largest and most innovative community colleges were in the Midwest (e.g., St. Louis, Milwaukee, Joliet, DuPage, Lorain, Cuyahoga, Sinclair, Macomb, Henry Ford).

Educating Knowledge Workers for a New Knowledge Economy

The current economic base and opportunity structure have changed from this industrial heyday. Our learning institutions must now be redefined to take advantage of opportunities that are consonant with the new global information-based economy.

Fast-forward to today: What are the educational imperatives of the emergent global knowledge-based economy? What are the dynamics of this great third wave of movement in the dominant strata of employment from farm to factory, to knowledge services conducted in offices, laboratories, hospitals, and classrooms, and centered on customer relations? And won't we still have to make things—particularly in the Midwest, with its manufacturing base? The answer is *yes*, but we will require fewer people. Like agriculture before it, manufacturing will and can remain an important economic contributor, but it will be increasingly automated, technically sophisticated, and supported by other jobs in design, engineering, and marketing, and quite different from the direct fabrication of products.

This knowledge economy is one that is truly global. Years before Thomas Friedman (2005) told us "The World Is Flat," Drucker (1994) pointed out that "knowledge knows no boundaries. There is no domestic knowledge and no international knowledge. There is only knowledge, and with knowledge becoming the key resource there is only a world economy."

The global economy is moving to the urbanized centers of idea exchange, trade, and traffic. The world just passed a tipping point where over half of its population now lives in urbanized areas. The Internet has accelerated the centralization of work, versus the decentralization pattern many predicted. As work is increasingly done from computers in offices, labs, and classrooms, people are enjoying the benefits of proximity to each other, as well as the ideas, culture, and other amenities of urban life.

As Drucker predicted, with the knowledge economy, educational institutions become the centerpoint of the economy. This reality is illustrated by the fact that college towns and cities, particularly those communities with research universities, are a dominant factor in creating new businesses and increased population density. All the emerging economic sectors (IT, bioscience, materials, energy) are growing in close proximity to research universities. Learning institutions are thus key contributors of place-defining economic attributes: they populate geographies and communities with very talented and educated people and they add culture, a centerpoint for community activities, and feed and support a diverse array of local businesses, arts, and entertainment. In turn, these communities become choice locations for lots of other people, some connected to the learning institution, but many not connected. One has to look no further than Madison, Wisconsin; Bloomington, Indiana; or Ann Arbor, Michigan, with their robust civic life and local culture and more vibrant economies, to see this dynamic at work. And the resurgence of former industrial communities like Pittsburgh and Cleveland can be directly linked to growing and leveraging their great research universities, Carnegie Mellon and Case Western Reserve.

As place-definers, learning institutions contribute to community values and culture, which in turn enhance their communities' attractiveness, making them magnets for mobile talent. University towns animate community attitudes—learning, and a culture that values learning, as well as tolerance and appreciation of diversity. These communities are also identified as places where people are working on vanguard issues—global sustainability, climate change, social justice—which again compounds their appeal to many young people. With all their cultural amenities, they also become destination spots for retirees and the booming number of longer-living empty-nesters.

While these place-specific attributes mean a boon for university towns, they also apply, if to a lesser degree, to community colleges in generating similar community benefits. In some communities, community colleges are the "only higher education institution in town" and can serve in university-like roles as cultural hubs and community convener catalysts.

There are a number of implications for the education, skills, and college preparation needed by the individuals who seek to navigate and succeed in this economy. In yesterday's economy, your most valuable commodity was the expensive equipment in your plant or the value of the land you owned. You kept the factory and office under lock and key, paid people who showed up and turned the screws or manned the phones, and replaced them readily if they didn't. In today's workplace, however, the most valuable commodity an employer has is the people in the organization and their knowledge assets: what they know, what they can do, and who they know. As Drucker (1994) put it,

> in the knowledge society, the employees, that is the knowledge workers, own the tools of production. In this new reality, you give your employees the key to the office and pray they will show up tomorrow, not leave you. The market researcher needs a computer, but increasingly this is the researcher's own personal computer, and it goes wherever he or she goes. The true capital equipment of market research is the knowledge of markets, of statistics, and of the application of market research to business strategy, which is lodged between the researcher's ears and is his or her exclusive and inalienable property.

In this economy credentials and skills become assets that help you, not merely to move up predictable career paths, but rather to rock-climb by moving from position to position to take advantage of new opportunities, armed with new skills and credentials and empowered by the social networks and contacts you develop along the way. Labor markets are totally contingent, and everyone is a free agent on their own behalf. There is no such thing as guaranteed lifetime employment, corporate or individual loyalty, or expectations of longevity.

What skills are needed by this dominant cadre of knowledge workers? Drucker describes the movement from the blue-collar industrial worker to a growing class of *technologists* (computer technicians, medical technicians, engineers, market researchers) with facility for flexible specialization—the ability to learn and apply highly specialized skills and to move rapidly from one job to another, such as from market research into management or from nursing into hospital administration.

He suggests this requires qualifications the industrial worker does not possess and is poorly equipped to acquire. This includes a very good formal education, as well as the ability to acquire and to apply theoretical and analytical knowledge on an ongoing basis, to develop habits of continuous learning, and to develop and apply new highly specialized skills in new situations.

Challenge and Opportunity for the Midwestern Education Institutions

These changes are enormously challenging for the Midwest, which has relied on the old paradigm of industrial organization. What does all this mean for the future of K-through-12, two-year, four-year, and research institutions? It means that an education system organized to well prepare the different cadres needed for the agro-industrial economy is out the window.

K-through-12 and high school reform includes ending the three-stream tracking of students into college preparatory, vocational-technical, and general education. As reflected in the new state Common Core Standards, this means creating a more engaging integrated learning experience with high expectations for all students to leave high school both college- and career-ready.

The two-year institution's role in this equation continues to evolve and blur with the roles of other institutions of higher education and to develop new ways of engaging the comprehensive community-focused missions. The role of local institutions to match regional labor market needs in rather narrow bands of technical capacity is now less significant. Local labor markets are less defined by durable careers and occupations to which the education system responds and more defined by what the education system and educated people create.

Technical and midlevel jobs still exist, and further education and specialized training is necessary but often insufficient to ensure success in the new labor market. Individuals need the tools to learn, learn again, adapt, navigate the labor market, identify new opportunities, and self-generate skills and credentials to enable them to seize or develop opportunities.

As is already evident, two-year and four-year institutions are morphing their functions. A growing number of community colleges have become low-cost way-stations that allow learners to transfer to four-year institutions and obtain the advanced degrees they believe give them a leg up in the marketplace. In this reality, community colleges are the accessible low-cost starter home, leading students toward the dream of higher education. Two-year colleges are an important entry mode into the human capital development system, also playing a particularly pivotal role with working-age adults who are either just beginning or rebooting their education, including older workers, immigrants, and single mothers.

Public Policy Implications

The major public policy implications involve using the new dynamics of the global knowledge economy to our advantage and building on the region's unrivaled learning infrastructure. With four priorities clearly and widely affirmed, we must capitalize on the conditions that can best animate new economic opportunity in the region.

A first priority is to fuel the research and learning centers of the Great Lakes–Midwest region as the innovation centers for the nation. Research and learning institutions are huge economic engines. They have significant spillover benefits, including new enterprise creation, knowledge transfer, and talent agglomeration.

As suggested in the "Vital Center" recommendations, a growing federal energy research-and-development activity was recently repurposed as a network of research university–hubbed Energy Innovation Institutes. Similarly, a significant portion of the federal America's Recovery and Reinvestment Act (ARRA) stimulus dollars dispensed over the past three years by the National Institutes of Health (NIH) and the Department of Energy Research has been awarded competitively to Midwestern research universities to expand the national capacity for new energy research. This should result in talent agglomeration and new commercial spillovers and spinoffs in the region. Moreover, the Midwest Governors agenda has been recently centered on advancing the Midwest's new energy economy. This initiative is anchored with a strong emphasis on developing the human and financial capital to commercialize innovation from the Midwest's energy research base.

A second major agenda for the region is to see the region's community colleges and universities better support and transform worker opportunities in the new free-agent, human capital marketplace. Toward this end, community colleges are adapting to new economic realities, by creating new bachelor and terminal degree options such as the applied baccalaureate. In addition, many are expanding their role as university centers for baccalaureate capstone program extensions from other institutions and providing a geographically and financially accessible avenue to degrees and skills essential in the knowledge economy. In another initiative, Midwest regional community

NEW DIRECTIONS FOR COMMUNITY COLLEGES • DOI: 10.1002/cc

colleges recently organized an Auto-Region community college consortium. Together they are applying for a share of the $2 billion Community College and Career Training Initiative announced by the Department of Labor, which has repurposed the Trade Adjustment Assistance monies to support locally defined workforce skill-building needs for a network of Midwestern communities sharing similar economic challenges.

In this emerging education marketplace, one in which serving free agents with relevant programs, offering private and public sector–relevant credentials, and competing with many new private providers has become the norm, community colleges are paying more attention to what the knowledge worker customer needs:

- Market-driven program options and more flexible hours
- Focus on completion of marketable credentials rather than enrichment
- Supports and services that allow emerging customer populations to succeed with rapid basic skill enhancement and attention to particular needs of minorities, women, immigrants, and other special populations

Four-year and graduate institutions are also adapting to changed economic realities in which they have an even more powerful role in this emergent knowledge economy as research and advanced learning centers. They have become the new idea incubators and technology innovation centers, as well as the talent generators for the new knowledge economy. Their job is less about preparing the managerial class and more about enhancing and extending the Midwest's multidisciplinary skill-building tool kit. Their research mission supports their knowledge sector specialties (e.g., stem-cell research, nanoscience, bio-fuels, or cyber-security) while sustaining a focus on preparing the "flexible specialists" for Drucker's knowledge economy.

A third priority for the region is to embrace new policies and practices, including but not limited to multistate and multi-institution tuition reciprocity and credit-transfer policies that help redefine the Midwest region as the place for talent generation—that is, a place for acquiring high-quality, competitively priced higher education degrees and skills of value. Advances on this front to define the region as the best market for learning will help keep our residents here, help them be better prepared, and reinvent the Midwest's role as educator of the world.

Finally, even in a time of seriously crimped state budgets, there are creative ways states can change budget priorities to support their emerging mission and the needs of the region. Amid the higher education cuts and rising tuition costs, public higher education institutions must focus on getting outcomes that matter: more degree completions and more basic research. Recently, Ohio policymakers have been holding higher education relatively harmless in budget cutting, but in return for putting in place a funding model that rewards institutions for completion of degrees, not seat-time. Indiana is matching federal research dollars won with state dollars, effectively piggybacking on high-quality research support. Michigan is looking to protect community colleges and to reallocate K-through-12 education funds to support community colleges given the important role they play in the economy. Essentially, this policy extends the K-through-12 system to one of expecting K-through-14 degrees and credentials for all youth and young adults.

While these policy initiatives are challenging to execute, they help to characterize the Midwest as the global education and innovation center. They involve repurposing the resources and institutions that made us great in the twentieth century and using them differently and strategically in the twenty-first century knowledge economy. In so doing, we can reanimate the great learning institutions we helped to invent—the land-grant public university and the community college—as engines of new economic opportunity. Without question, in the knowledge era these institutions are the centerpiece of our economy and culture.

References

Austin, J., and Affolter-Caine, B. "The Vital Center: A Federal-State Compact to Renew the Great Lakes Region." Washington, D.C.: Brookings Institution, 2006. Retrieved March 27, 2011, from http://www.brookings.edu/~/media/Files/rc/reports/2006/10metropolitanpolicy_austin/20061020_renewgreatlakes.pdf

Austin, J. C., Affolter-Caine, B. and Dezenski, E. "The Vital Connection: Reclaiming Great Lake Economic Leadership in the Bi-National U.S.-Canadian Region." Washington, D.C.: Brookings Institution, 2007. Retrieved March 27, 2011, from http://www.brookings.edu/~/media/Files/rc/reports/2008/0324_greatlakes_canada_austin/greatlakes_canada.pdf

Drucker, P. F. *Landmarks of Tomorrow.* New York: Harper, 1959.

Drucker, P. F. "The Age of Social Transformation." *Atlantic Monthly*, November 1994.

Jacobs, J. "The Federal Role in Leveraging America's Community Colleges." Washington, D.C.: Brookings Institution, 2010. Retrieved March 28, 2011, from http://www.brookings.edu/~/media/Files/rc/papers/2010/0927_great_lakes/0927_great_lakes_papers/0927_great_lakes_community_college.pdf

Friedman, Thomas L. *The World is Flat: A Brief History of the 21st Century.* New York: Farrar, Straus and Giroux, 2005.

Longworth, R. C. *Caught in the Middle: America's Heartland in the Age of Globalism.* New York: Bloomsbury, 2008.

The Northwest Ordinance, Article III. Retrieved March 29, 2011, from http://teachingamericanhistory.org/library/index.asp?document=48

Vey, J. S., Austin, J. C., and Bradley, J. "The Next Economy: Economic Recovery and Transformation in the Great Lakes Region." Washington, D.C.: Brookings Institution, 2010. Retrieved March 28, 2011, from http://www.brookings.edu/papers/2010/0927_great_lakes.aspx

JOHN AUSTIN is president of the Michigan State Board of Education. In addition, he is a nonresident senior fellow at the Brookings Institution and co-director of the Great Lakes Economic Initiative.

NEW DIRECTIONS FOR COMMUNITY COLLEGES • DOI: 10.1002/cc

3

This chapter provides a case study on how thirteen institutions of higher education, ten of which are community colleges, created a blueprint for successful regional collaboration on critical education and economic challenges.

Building Regional Economic Growth and Innovation Capacity

H. Jeffrey Rafn

Overview

Like many states at the turn of the century, Wisconsin was faced with a multibillion-dollar deficit due to a sagging economy brought on by the dot-com bubble burst and the economic impact of the 9/11 terrorist attack on the World Trade Center. As the state legislature grappled with the budget crisis, blame was freely assigned. The state was at fault for building in structural deficits in the prior years, not setting aside sufficient rainy-day funds, and creating unfunded mandates that pushed costs onto local governments (city, county, schools). Localities were at fault for wasteful spending, inordinate compensation and health insurance costs, redundant services, and having an unsustainable number of local jurisdictions. The manufacturing industry, upon which Wisconsin relied heavily, had failed to properly prepare for the next generation of technology, had made poor management decisions resulting in loss of profitability, had not adopted "lean" practices, and was ill-equipped to compete in the global market.

While all of these factors and others undoubtedly played a part in the financial challenges faced by Wisconsin, the assignment of blame did nothing to address the long-term implications of these issues. A 2001 report by the Wisconsin Governor's Blue Ribbon Commission on State–Local Partnerships for the twenty-first century, commonly referred to as the *Kettle Commission Report*, noted that a high quality of life in twenty-first-century Wisconsin depended on the state defining and nurturing its regions. It

New Directions for Community Colleges, no. 157, Spring 2012 © 2012 Wiley Periodicals, Inc.
Published online in Wiley Online Library (wileyonlinelibrary.com) • DOI: 10.1002/cc.20004

urged the state to create strong incentives for local governments in each region to work collaboratively to make the region stronger. This call for regionalism was reinforced by a series of statewide economic summits initiated by the University of Wisconsin (UW) System (see http://www .wisconsin.edu/summit/). In turn, these summits spawned regional economic summits, which attracted a diverse set of actors spanning government, business, and education. In Northeast Wisconsin, the conversations that ensued led to a period of regional collaboration previously unseen.

Northeast Wisconsin as a geographical region is composed of eighteen counties stretching from Fond du Lac County in the south to Florence County in the north and Marquette and Waupaca Counties in the west to Manitowoc and Sheboygan on the shores of Lake Michigan. With a population of 1.2 million, it contains a mix of agricultural, forestry, and manufacturing businesses. It is second only to Milwaukee in its concentration of manufacturing with its historical basis in paper and paper-related businesses along the Fox River. Today, manufacturing is fairly well diversified with a strong presence in ship and boat building, automotive parts, food production, and machine and machine parts fabrication. Several major health systems, insurance firms, banks, and other service firms call this area home. A common cultural history, commuting patterns, and educational attainment further cement this area into a region.

The balance of this chapter will describe two of the most influential and enduring regional collaborations to come out of this period: the Northeast Wisconsin Educational Resource Alliance (NEWERA) and New North. NEWERA is the precursor to the creation of New North and in many ways influenced its development. Lessons and insights from this case study are provided.

The Northeast Wisconsin Education Resource Alliance (NEWERA)

No initiative of this magnitude can begin without dedicated leadership and vision. With the catalyst of the Kettle Commission Report and the university-hosted economic summits, the chancellor of the University of Wisconsin–Oshkosh and the president of Northeast Wisconsin Technical College provided the leadership and vision that brought together the presidents and chancellors of the thirteen postsecondary public education institutions in Northeast Wisconsin, a region later deemed the "New North." This group consisted of two comprehensive universities (UW–Green Bay and UW–Oshkosh), four Wisconsin technical colleges (WTCs) (Fox Valley, Lakeshore, Moraine Park, and Northeast), five associate degree–granting transfer campuses of the University of Wisconsin Colleges (Fox Valley, Fond du Lac, Manitowoc, Marinette, and Sheboygan), the College of Menominee Nation, and the University of Wisconsin Extension.

NEW DIRECTIONS FOR COMMUNITY COLLEGES • DOI: 10.1002/cc

In 2001, when NEWERA was established, the environment within public higher education reflected distrust, competition, and academic elitism among the institutions. The historically agreed-upon roles of each type of institution were under assault as the public demanded greater transferability between and among the institutions; students were developing workarounds that allowed them to transfer credits, and the rigor and breadth of education needed by students in technical fields traditionally addressed in technical colleges grew. Within the University of Wisconsin System, the University of Wisconsin Colleges' campuses competed with the comprehensive and research universities for funding, often feeling they were the last to receive resources and attention. As the technical colleges responded to demands by employers for workers who could communicate well, lead, solve problems, think analytically, work in teams, and be creative and innovative, the rigor and amount of education students needed in communication, physical and social sciences, and mathematics in addition to the technical skills of the field in which they were enrolled were increased. This blurring of the lines between what was offered in the first two years of higher education and the WTCs' associate degree programs fueled the demand by students, the public, and employers for technical college education to be recognized as transferable to the universities. Given that the technical colleges have more than five times the full-time equivalent enrollment in associate degree programs than the university colleges (53,222 vs. 8,909 in 2008–2009), that they account for more transfers into the universities, and that their reliance on property taxes for 57 percent of their revenue is more secure than state funding, it is little wonder that this blurring of the lines has been perceived as a threat by some on the University of Wisconsin Colleges' campuses. The competition for limited state funding merely exacerbated the tensions among the public higher education institutions.

NEWERA sought to overcome these tensions by persistently encouraging collaboration and cooperation between the public higher education institutions. To be sure, the first few meetings were characterized by subtle and not-so-subtle accusations and finger-pointing. From the beginning, however, all parties believed in the higher purpose of meeting the needs of the region through collaboration. It was hard work, and critical to the success of this endeavor was the emergence of a champion from each of the three major systems: technical colleges, universities, and university college campuses. The champions' commitment, belief, and passion for the importance and necessity of regional collaboration served as a constant source of energy and inspiration to overcome the many obstacles to true collaboration. The champions worked at getting their colleagues to attend the meetings, ensured that controversial issues were put on the table, and engaged the appropriate staff in resolving issues.

Within the first year, NEWERA was able to agree on a mission and vision statement. Its mission was to act as a consortium that fosters regional partnerships among the thirteen public colleges and universities in

Northeast Wisconsin (hereafter referred to as "New North") to better serve the educational needs of the 1.2 million people in Northeast Wisconsin. NEWERA's vision was to become a national leader in collaborating to accomplish the following:

- Serve Northeast Wisconsin with quality seamless education.
- Provide essential educational resources for communities, businesses, and government.
- Drive regional, and thereby state, economic vitality.

It was determined that the chair of NEWERA would rotate every two years, moving from the universities to the technical colleges to the university college campuses, thereby ensuring shared leadership from all three systems. For the first four years, however, the chair was the chancellor of UW–Oshkosh. Given the fragile nature of the organization during the first two years, this provided some important stability. There were no dues, and financial obligations taken on by NEWERA were shared by each member or volunteered by one of the members. The chair engaged his or her executive assistant in recording minutes, arranging meeting logistics, and otherwise following up on actions taken by NEWERA.

It was very important that NEWERA have some early successes in order to increase the investment of the institutional leadership in pursuing collaboration and demonstrating to the community that public higher education could successfully work together. To this end, a NEWERA library card was developed through the collaboration of the NEWERA library directors. By obtaining one of these cards, students could freely use any of the libraries in NEWERA. The first card was presented to the Governor of Wisconsin and the event was widely promoted throughout the libraries. A second project was to create a trailing spouse program. A brochure was developed and a Web site was established that allowed spouses of persons relocating to the region to work at one of the NEWERA institutions to easily search for work at any of the other NEWERA institutions. These initial successes gave the NEWERA leaders some breathing room to work on the more difficult issues of program transfer, resource sharing, and collaborative program development without some of the political interference both within and outside the systems.

After the creation of the mission and vision statements, annual retreats ensued. Three recurring retreat goals were identified:

1. Advance the economic vitality of the region and the quality of life it supports.
2. Utilize NEWERA collaborations to continue to learn from each other and to generate internal stakeholder commitment and support.
3. Optimize access and maximize the ability of the public to navigate among NEWERA institutions.

While these goals have stayed constant throughout the life of NEWERA, the goals have been revisited and action steps have been changed each year. Accomplishments in collaborative academic and technical programs have been many, including creation of: (1) three engineering programs, (2) an Alcohol and Other Drug Abuse (AODA) associate degree with the College of Menominee Nation, (3) a one-plus-three general education certificate at the technical colleges, allowing for direct transfer into the NEWERA universities as sophomores, and (4) several bachelor's degree completion programs available to all associate of applied sciences graduates. Additional accomplishments include: professional development forums on adult learning and services, a university center at a technical college, annual legislative breakfasts, and a faculty dialogue group. These last two are particularly important.

Unlike many breakfasts held for legislators, this breakfast was designed around reporting results of NEWERA's efforts, not the need for increased funding. Early on, NEWERA leaders adopted a core value of public accountability by reporting the plans it was accomplishing. Each year a point was made to report on any action taken regarding the concerns raised earlier. By modeling the benefits of regional collaboration, it was hoped that NEWERA could assist New North legislators in working as a coalition, thereby increasing the political influence of the region at the state and federal levels.

To engage the regional issues of mutual concern, working groups led by champions were appointed to strengthen regional collaboration buy-in at the campus level. In 2005 a faculty dialogue group was established. Each NEWERA member institution provided one or two faculty to serve as members of the group. Initially, appointment was to be made for two years; later, at the request of the faculty, members were allowed to serve a third year. Terms were staggered, the group chose its own chair, and it established its own action plan in alignment with the overall goals of NEWERA.

The faculty dialogue was formed in recognition that faculty members were central in establishing mutually respectful relationships among the NEWERA institutions, leading to the recognition and transfer of credit. The group was charged with assisting in the development of a more seamless higher education environment for students among the NEWERA institutions. Specifically, it was asked to:

- Identify and clarify interinstitutional collaboration issues among the University of Wisconsin and Wisconsin Technical College systems.
- Explore teaching and curriculum in the UW and WTC systems, particularly in relation to credit transfer potential.
- Recommend specific strategies, activities, and events to build stronger relationships among the faculty of the NEWERA institutions.

The accomplishments of this group are many, but the most significant is the relationship-building that has occurred among its members. The mutual respect and understanding created through these relationships have made the task of creating transfer and recognition of credit much easier. The rotation of faculty dialogue group members has enlarged the shared understanding of the high caliber of education provided on each campus and sparked a level of intra- and interinstitutional collaboration that continues to grow. Conversations regarding collaborative program development, adult education, alternative learning delivery methods, and pre-college preparation programs are no longer met with rancorous debate about the quality of each institution or the degrees held by faculty. Rather, the discussion focused on transfer, advising, and maximizing student success.

As NEWERA neared its tenth anniversary in 2010, two different work groups were created: one to explore and make recommendations on establishing baccalaureate-level engineering technology programs that included enabling the first two years to be completed at either the UW Colleges' or technical colleges' campuses, and the second to develop a plan and recommendations that would position NEWERA as a leader in the provision of sustainability-related programming. Once these reports were completed, it immediately became evident that they called for a sharing of capital and operational resources yet to be seen. Moreover, the success of these two initiatives would require technical colleges to open their campuses for use by the universities; the joint development and ownership of curriculum among the technical colleges, the universities, and the UW college campuses; and the combined political influence of all member institutions to overcome internal and external obstacles. It was clear that NEWERA's previous manner of funding initiatives on an ad-hoc basis would no longer work. At a minimum, a dedicated professional would be needed to sustain and grow these efforts.

Meanwhile, the NEWERA institutions were feeling the effects of the severe recession of 2009–2010. Enrollments had climbed dramatically as dislocated workers and high school graduates opted for more education when they could not find jobs. Without any significant increase in state funding and the concurrent decline in property valuation that supported the technical colleges, the NEWERA members were scrambling to meet this expanded demand with limited resources. At the very moment when the need to share resources was at its highest, NEWERA had the least capability of doing so.

Discussion ensued as to the need to hire an executive director and provide an ongoing source of financial support. The strength of ten years of collaboration was reflected in the fact that the group could agree on the responsibilities of the executive director and an annual budget of $200,000. Further, NEWERA agreed to become an incorporated nonprofit entity to which these funds would be allocated for an annual program of work. Collectively, the local WTCs' presidents and the UW System each committed $100,000 annually for three years to sustain the vital NEWERA regional innovation capacity.

Sustaining NEWERA has had and will continue to have its challenges. During its formative years and its continued existence the often-underground debate regarding the nature and structure of higher education in the state of Wisconsin has continued unabated. Changes in leadership and actions taken by the University of Wisconsin Colleges created the suspicion that the college leadership wanted to take on some of the work historically viewed by the technical colleges as its domain. Unsubstantiated rumors within both systems that one was positioning to take over the other persisted. The expressed desire by the UW Colleges to offer in a limited fashion a baccalaureate degree caused concern among the universities. When a technical college on the other side of the state sought and received permission to offer a two-year liberal arts transfer degree, some saw this as the beginning of a process leading eventually to all of the technical colleges offering this degree, to the detriment of the UW Colleges.

Since the NEWERA launch, the state policy landscape has been, as in other states, filled with debates about transfer, baccalaureate expansion, and financial aid support. Keeping all of this noise at bay while pursuing its own plans required NEWERA's members to hold candid discussions regarding each member's position on a number of these issues. NEWERA leadership testified before the University Board of Regents and the Wisconsin Technical College System Board of Trustees asking for the flexibility to try new approaches without interference from the system offices. By keeping the noise at bay, NEWERA has been and is recognized by the university and technical systems as having made significant progress in establishing strong collaborations that have in turn strengthened both systems and improved the experience of regionally mobile students in higher education. The capacity for sustaining challenging conversations among the NEWERA members is central to maintaining a productive regional relationship while the noise continues unabated.

The keys to the success of NEWERA were simple yet challenging to implement. First and foremost was the need for perseverance. Various members often wondered whether NEWERA was ever going to accomplish anything other than talk. At different times, some members had to work with other, disillusioned members in order to keep them engaged. Collaboration is hard work and finding the willingness to stick with the process can be difficult. Frank and candid conversations that build moderate levels of trust are essential. Once the members realized that what they said would be held confidentially and would not be used in negative ways, real progress was made. Getting to this point took at least a year and meant being willing to call out violators. Early successes created the momentum to persevere and the faith that the process of collaboration was worth the effort. CEOs could do nothing alone. Those who were tasked with doing the work had to be engaged in the goal-setting and planning behind that work. In the end, faculty were and are the key to an institution's success, just as they are to the students' success. Strategies had to be in place to gain their input, investment, and action.

As NEWERA enters its second decade, it promises to accomplish ever-more-challenging goals contributing to the economic and educational strength of the colleges and New North.

NEWERA and the Development of New North

In many ways, NEWERA was the foundation on which the New North initiative was built. It demonstrated the benefits of regional collaboration and served as a model for how collaboration could be achieved without giving up the identity of each partner. With near-similar geographic boundaries, the New North was created in 2003–2004 to revitalize and enhance other regional economic collaborations, including (1) the Northeast Wisconsin Regional Economic Partnership (NEWREP), which included economic development directors throughout the region; (2) the longstanding Cooperative Educational Service Agencies (CESAs) serving the primary and secondary public education districts; (3) the two workforce development organizations created through the federal Workforce Investment Act (WIA); (4) a nascent chamber network among the four major cities on the Fox River (Green Bay, Appleton, Oshkosh, and Fond du Lac); and (5) the Bay Lake and East Central Planning Commissions. None of these collaborations was as expansive as NEWERA in the regions they covered.

Commissioned by the Bay Area and Fox Valley Workforce Development Boards, the *Northeast Wisconsin Economic Opportunity Study* (Winters and Ward, 2004) was conducted by NorthStar Economics Inc. The purpose of the study was to determine how to "halt the deteriorating employment trends" of the region and to provide a roadmap for creating a more prosperous, growing economy. Its premise was that the new economy is based on ideas, creativity, and innovation. The driving premise was that successful businesses will move to where the skilled and professional labor resides. To achieve the new regional economy, five strategies, composed of ninety-eight actions steps, were recommended. Later, in the fall of 2004, a summit (the first annual) involving leaders throughout Northeast Wisconsin was held in Green Bay with Richard Florida (2005), author of *The Rise of the Creative Class*, as the keynote speaker. It was here that many were first introduced to the notion of the new economy being the creative economy. The recommendations of the study and this summit served as the impetus for the creation of New North.

Three events occurred in the early part of 2005 that helped to establish the present New North structure. First, a group of business CEOs called together by area chambers of commerce began a process to create a regional brand and to help implement the recommendations of the economic opportunity study. Two strong, passionate private-sector leaders emerged from the group and provided the driving force and the means to create New North. In January 2005, the second event occurred when an organizing committee was established with the task of creating an organizational structure to initiate and oversee the implementation of economic and workforce development recommendations. The institutional NEWERA leaders played a significant role in shaping the charter for this organization. Three NEWERA leaders were able to moderate the sometimes-delicate conversations that ensued among the stakeholders as each sought to protect their own interests while creating the necessary collaboration to achieve the recommendations of the economic opportunity study. The third event was the acquisition of a grant from the Wisconsin Department of Commerce, which allowed for the initial funding stability to attract an executive director for New North. Further, the commitment of the Department of Commerce bolstered the work of the business CEOs and the area chambers in raising funds from other businesses and community partners. The NEWERA partnership agreed to become one of the significant contributors, making a three-year commitment, followed by a subsequent three-year commitment. The fact that NEWERA contributed as a single entity rather than as separate colleges modeled the way a regional collaboration could work.

At the second annual summit in December 2005, the new brand, "New North: North of What You Expect," was rolled out and the new executive director was introduced. Shared vision, mission, and values were adopted. Desired measurable outcomes were agreed on. Now in its sixth year, New North has a budget of approximately $1,000,000 and over seventy contributors, the vast majority being private-sector businesses. The organization consists of a board of directors, an executive committee, and committees on finance and fundraising as well as board development. There are six strategy teams, one for each major strategic initiative identified in the *Northeast Economic Opportunities Report*. Of the six strategic initiatives, two focus on the development and recruitment of talent, three on business development, and one on marketing and recruitment.

Of the two strategic teams addressing talent development and recruitment, one is working to attract, develop, and retain diverse talent and the other is focused on encouraging educational attainment. NEWERA has been particularly active on the latter team, which is chaired by a NEWERA member. Staff members from several NEWERA member institutions serve on the team and the various sub-teams. Many of the NEWERA accomplishments listed earlier were reported as accomplishments of New North. This collective reporting strategy proved useful in demonstrating the critical interface of regional education and workforce development priorities, as well as documenting public accountability for the stakeholders. The current focus of the Educational Attainment team is as follows:

- Develop model curriculum that integrates twenty-first century skills.
- Devise strategies to overcome the achievement gap and begin pilot programs.
- Establish a plan and timeline for the implementation of needed engineering programs.

- Optimize job- and career-matching tools on a regional basis.
- Provide strategies to businesses on how to engage in partnerships with educators.

Given the severe economic issues within the region, *pursuing targeted growth opportunities* is the first of three strategic business development initiatives—all of which have education and workforce training implications. Some of the strategies include:

- Sustain and grow the maritime shipbuilding industry.
- Continue the development of the wind sector cluster.
- Develop the modernized agribusiness sector cluster.
- Develop the cellulosic ethanol sector cluster.
- Develop the Web-based manufacturing sector cluster.
- Support and promote the Manufacturers' Alliance.
- Create economic development strategies for rural regions in New North.

Within each of these strategies, NEWERA leaders have been active participants in credit and noncredit program development. A sampling of the joint efforts includes: (1) developing an associate degree in wind technology, (2) providing education on the production of bio-diesel, (3) creating a new degree program and courses in organic farming, and (4) establishing a Manufacturing Engineering program through a partnership with a New North technical college and a state university outside the region. Finally, NEWERA members were key partners with a New North shipbuilding company's success in receiving a multimillion-dollar defense contract. The two-year colleges will provide essential training and education to the more than one thousand additional workers that will be hired.

A second business-development strategic initiative is to *support an entrepreneurial climate and the growth of small businesses*. This team has focused on creating entrepreneurial networks, providing education, and finding capital. NEWERA members have heavily supported these efforts, since the universities and colleges are major providers of entrepreneurial education and the business practices needed in order to be successful. Several of the technical colleges and universities in New North, in collaboration with business partners, provide incubating space and startup services for new businesses.

The third strategic initiative in business development is relatively new and centers on *adopting sustainable practices*. A number of NEWERA institutions have completed sustainability plans for their own physical plants and have committed to reducing their carbon footprints. The process of integrating sustainable-practice knowledge across the curriculum of all programs has begun in many of the colleges and universities. NEWERA charged its campus champions of resource sustainability to jointly develop a plan that provides the education programming and technical services, community action, and research needed to make New North the number-one region in the country in adopting sustainable practices. This plan is in place and being pursued under the leadership of NEWERA's executive director.

Each year the New North strategic teams, which are staffed almost exclusively by volunteers, establish plans and measurable goals. In December of each year an annual half-day summit is held in a New North community, and draws over eight hundred business, government, and educational leaders. Summit attendees review the prior year's accomplishments and preview future plans. Similar to the NEWERA practice, a visible commitment to annual public accountability has leveraged a wide spectrum of partner engagement and collective action. Moreover, these strategic task forces and reports have increased investor confidence in the organization and solidified its funding support.

Many challenges face the New North organization as it continues to grow and mature. The organization struggles with maintaining the desired balance between being a service organization, a catalyst for collaboration, and an agent for economic development. It continues to refine its use of metrics to demonstrate a return on investment. Generating sufficient financial support may always be a challenge, especially in a sluggish recovery period. Reaching and engaging the rural areas of New North has proven particularly difficult. New North, by design, has a staff of only two or three people. As a catalyst for collaboration, it does its work through others. While this helps maintain positive relations with those who may otherwise view the New North organization as a competitor, it calls into question how much can be done with such a limited staff. NEWERA leadership will undoubtedly be key to New North's successfully meeting these challenges.

Whereas the recession of 2009–2010 negatively impacted many of the members of New North, at no time did the need for and the continued support of New North diminish. In fact, Wisconsin's then-Governor Doyle touted New North as an example of how regional collaboration can work. He included the creation of regional economic collaborations as one of his eight strategic goals in his plan, "Grow Wisconsin: Accelerate-Innovate, Building the Next Generation of Wisconsin Industry" (Doyle, 2008). Using New North as a model, his administration made awards to seven regional economic development organizations across the state.

Governor Scott Walker has taken it a step further by reorganizing the state's Department of Commerce, creating a private–public partnership akin to New North. He appointed the chief executive of the Green Bay Area Chamber of Commerce to be his Secretary of Commerce. Since this person was a major proponent of New North, much of his experience will inform the development of this new partnership. With a four-to-five-year head start in addressing regional postsecondary education priorities, NEWERA paved the way for the creation of these regional economic collaborations, and without question community and technical colleges are key players in each of these partnerships.

Conclusion

Throughout the development and implementation of the work of New North, it is apparent that the NEWERA colleges and universities were essential to the success of this economic development initiative. NEWERA's financial support came not only as cash but as in-kind donations, including leadership, research and planning, printing and design, and information technology support. Most importantly, the presence of an eighteen-county higher education network served to validate the potential success of such a geographically expansive initiative. The work of NEWERA gave New North the early successes needed to inspire public and investor support. NEWERA's willingness to create alignment between its initiatives and New North's own initiatives brought essential resources to the effort. NEWERA's annual legislative breakfasts modeled the accountability to which New North holds itself.

As two-year higher education institutions in the Midwest respond to the economic and demographic changes in the region, NEWERA provides an excellent example of how collaboration among all public higher education institutions can provide the leadership needed to address these changes and drive the region toward a robust future. Perseverance, frank and candid discussion to build trust, early successes, and engaging faculty serve as the foundation. The need for continued collaboration has never been greater. Overcoming recent severe reductions in state and local funding, which are commonplace these days, will require greater integration of resources and leaders with strategically complementary rather than competing goals. The urge for each college to compete with others for an ever-diminishing pot of higher education public revenue must be vigorously resisted. Community colleges and their higher education colleagues have the opportunity to lead the nation in designing the new educational and economic development approaches needed to successfully compete in the global, twenty-first-century market. We must make the most of strategically aligned and leveraged approaches!

References

Doyle, J. (ed.). "Grow Wisconsin: Accelerate-Innovate, Building the Next Generation of Wisconsin Industry." December 2008. Retrieved November 17, 2009, from http://www.wisgov.state.wi.us/docview.asp?docid=12937

Florida, R. (2005). *The Flight of the Creative Class: The New Global Competition for Talent*. New York: Harper Collins.

Schejbal, D. *UW Colleges Annual Report for FY09*. Madison: University of Wisconsin Colleges, 2010.

State Fact Book for 2008–2009. Retrieved January 22, 2011, from http://www.wisconsin
.edu/cert/publicat/archive/factbook2008.pdf

Winters, D., and Ward, D. *Northeast Wisconsin Economic Opportunity Study.* Madison:
NorthStar Economics, 2004.

"Wisconsin Blue Ribbon Commission on State–Local Partnerships for the 21st Century."
January 2001. Retrieved January 22, 2011, from www.lafollette.wisc.edu

H. Jeffrey Rafn, *Ph.D., is president of Northeast Wisconsin Technical College
in Green Bay, Wisconsin, and a founding member of NEWERA.*

New Directions for Community Colleges • DOI: 10.1002/cc

4

This chapter explores how technological innovation is changing the kinds of skills and knowledge used in the workplace and how two-year colleges are responding to these changes. It features examples of new and emerging practices in Wisconsin's technical colleges that situate learning in settings designed to meet the needs of learners and their communities.

Learning and the New Workplace: Impacts of Technology Change on Postsecondary Career and Technical Education

Janet L. Washbon

The experience of technology change pervades our lives. Sometimes it comes in the guise of a new smart phone, e-reader, or patch for a leaky artery. Other times, it appears as a new way to track packages, connect with others through social networks, or find our way around an unfamiliar place. Or it reveals itself as a new surgical technique, way of organizing a factory or workplace, or diagnostic procedure. In short, technology change can range from devices that increase productivity or enhance communications, entertainment, or physical well-being to systems that bring people and information together to solve everyday problems, or tools that help us manipulate materials, structure work, or organize information and concepts.

In each case, technology change alters the way we apply knowledge and skills to control and adapt to our environment. Just as our own lives are not immune to the impacts of technology change, neither are workplace or education settings. This paper explores how technology change is reshaping our workplaces, the educational needs of our labor force, and the two-year colleges that provide career and technical education in the United States.

New Directions for Community Colleges, no. 157, Spring 2012 © 2012 Wiley Periodicals, Inc.
Published online in Wiley Online Library (wileyonlinelibrary.com) • DOI: 10.1002/cc.20005

The Changing American Workplace and Changing Skill Needs

Over the past thirty years, the development and use of office automation and business process technologies, together with commercialization of the Internet and the development of Web-based applications and computer-based telecommunications technologies, have transformed information retrieval and information sharing, both within and between organizations. The impact of these applications is changing the nature of work in industries as diverse as logistics, financial services, entertainment, health care, and education, as described by the U.S. Bureau of Labor Statistics (2005) and the U.S. Department of Labor (1999).

The use of geographic information systems, satellite communication, and microprocessors, for example, has transformed the field of logistics. Interstate truck stops are no longer just a place to rest, fuel up, and compare travel conditions, but offer truckers opportunities to log into the terminal to provide progress reports or check on-screen listings of the availability of new loads. Onboard scan tools communicate via satellite to provide fleet maintenance technicians with real-time information about truck performance and permits them to troubleshoot from a distance and determine the best way to perform maintenance. These tools can also provide real-time information on truck-driving performance such as speed, energy consumption, and shifting behaviors for driver-logistics feedback.

Similar examples from other fields abound. The recent interest in renewable energy, for example, is beginning to transform power generation and distribution, resulting in the need for technicians who can monitor and maintain the increasingly complex flows between multiple user-producers and existing techniques in the installation, operation, and maintenance of new technologies. In production agriculture, onboard computers teamed with equipment-specific sensors and global positioning technology permit farmers to monitor crop production and adjust planting, cultivation, and nutrient management to maximize yield. Entrepreneurs and managers in fields such as hospitality, retail sales and marketing, and barbering/cosmetology use database applications to manage their client base, tracking visits, services, and products to better target marketing and services to their clientele.

In each of these cases, the newly introduced technology is not simply a substitute for existing technology; it is transformative in changing core occupational practices. Its full integration in the workplace has changed the technical, cognitive, and behavioral skills employers seek in the labor market. Not only is a high school diploma viewed as insufficient preparation for work; even in economic downturns, many employers are seeking workers with the specific technical knowledge and skills typically gained in postsecondary educational programs, as noted by Handel (2005). In addition, employers expect workers to possess strong foundational skills such as the ability to communicate effectively, understand and appreciate diver-

NEW DIRECTIONS FOR COMMUNITY COLLEGES • DOI: 10.1002/cc

sity, demonstrate global awareness and sensitivity, work cooperatively, set and achieve goals, value themselves, model responsible behavior, learn effectively, apply relevant technologies, think critically and creatively, and access and use appropriate information resources (Partnership for 21st Century Skills, 2004).

In the face of these wide-ranging changes, the key question for policy-makers and educators alike is not just what kinds of skills, knowledge, and abilities are needed in the new American workplace, but how we can align educational institutions at the secondary and postsecondary level with workplace needs to ensure that workers are prepared for initial employ-ment and over the course of their lifetimes.

Reshaping Postsecondary Career and Technical Education

One way community and technical colleges have responded to the technol-ogy changes in the workplace is by significantly expanding opportunities for postsecondary preparation for work and skill upgrading. Although it is only one facet of the complex mission of community and technical col-leges, about three-fifths of the four million students enrolled annually in credit programs are pursuing career and technical education (Jacobs and Dougherty, 2006). This shift from college transfer to occupational prepara-tion has resulted in increased efforts at two-year colleges to determine what kinds of occupational programs are needed in their labor market, which of these many competing needs these colleges can best meet, and how to ensure that the curriculum offered in the programs can meet the needs of students, their employers, and their communities.

Anticipating and Meeting Programming Needs. Labor market information provides one obvious source of data about the training needs of regional labor markets. Since the mid-1980s, federal and most state labor departments have produced projections of labor demand by occupation that are updated on a two- or three-year cycle. These projections provide estimates of future employment growth and job openings based on assump-tions about industry staffing patterns and economic growth. Coupled with sophisticated resources such as O*Net Online, the federal occupational information database providing comprehensive information on key attri-butes and characteristics of workers and occupations, these projections can provide indications of the kinds of occupational programs that will be needed in an area and the types of skills, knowledge, and abilities students will need to find work in these fields.

Unfortunately, labor market projections are of limited use in identify-ing new and emerging occupations or changing skill needs within existing occupations. New and emerging occupations are by definition ones that have not existed or that have not been recognized as discrete occupations in the past. Webmasters, to take a familiar example, are not computer tech-nicians, marketers, or communications specialists. Instead, their jobs typi-

NEW DIRECTIONS FOR COMMUNITY COLLEGES • DOI: 10.1002/cc

cally combine some of the skills associated with each of these occupations and apply them to a new context: creating and managing the information content and organization of a Web site and managing its computer server and technical programming aspects. Wind energy technicians, to take a less familiar example, assemble, maintain, and repair wind turbines used in energy generation. Jobs in this field apply the skills associated with power line installation, repair, and maintenance to the unique requirements and settings of wind turbine technology, turbine maintenance, tower safety, and wind economics.

Labor market information programs provide little or no information about the demand for webmasters or wind energy technicians because the existing classification schemes recognize neither these nor other new and emerging occupations as separate from other related categories of jobs. Instead, community and technical colleges must build and rely on strong relationships with their employer base to help them understand and anticipate changes in the education and training needs of their community. National or state trends are important, but well-designed employer surveys, industry-based advisory committees, and targeted focus-group discussions with the college's employer community can provide more accurate and useful sources of information about regional demand in new and emerging occupations, changes in the content of established occupations, and the need to modify or even eliminate current programs.

Community and Technical College Responses.   Based on information drawn from these sources, community and technical college leaders are using a variety of techniques to identify and launch programs for new and emerging occupations. Some rely on developing sub-tracks within a new or existing program to meet specific demands for new and emerging occupations while ensuring that enrollments in core-related courses will make the overall program financially viable. Others share an existing curriculum developed by another college to meet emerging local demand. Yet another group relies on bundling a unique set of skills and knowledge drawn from multiple existing programs into short-term or certificate programs to test the labor market demand for separate degree or diploma programs. In each case, the colleges are trying to balance the employer-expressed desire for program graduates with other expressions of labor market demand to assure placement of graduates.

Innovative Community Partnerships for Skill Development.   At the same time that technological innovation is continually changing the mix of postsecondary career and technical education programs offered by two-year colleges, it is also changing how instruction is delivered and what is taught. Although classroom-based instruction is still the norm, most two-year colleges offer a variety of flexible learning options to meet the needs of working adults, many made possible by innovations in telecommunications. These include traditional distance education modes such as interactive television, videoconferencing, video-based delivery, and online learning as well as accelerated, self-paced, or weekend learning options. More recently, colleges have introduced hybrid instruction that permits students to attend class in the classroom or online depending on their work schedules or other commitments.

Community and technical colleges have long worked collaboratively with business and industry to develop curriculums and secure the equipment and related resources needed to deliver career and technical education programs that respond to the changing skill needs of workplaces. Many of these programs have included work-based learning or clinic placement components and incorporated industry standards to ensure that program graduates attain the skills needed in the workplace.

Four model partnerships that move beyond these now-standard practices to situate learning in settings that meet the needs of communities and learners are described in the following. What is common to each of these examples is that each of the colleges is actively collaborating with employers and their community to ensure that the instruction they offer helps students gain the technical, cognitive, analytical, and interpersonal skills needed to succeed in the modern workplace. Each also incorporates certification of technical skill attainment, either through nationally recognized standards and assessments, as is common in the health or public safety occupations, or through voluntary incorporation and assessment of industry standards developed by national groups such as the Manufacturing Skill Standards Council (2009).

Center for Manufacturing and Engineering Technology at Northeast Wisconsin Technical College. This center provides interdisciplinary instruction in manufacturing technology programs in a modular open-entry, instructor-assisted format. Thirteen defined learning centers provide students with access to self-paced, hands-on learning in hydraulics, pneumatics, mechanics, rigging, electronics, microprocessors, communications, motors, drives, control systems, servo mechanisms, programmable logic controllers, and human–machine interface with dedicated, state-of-the-art equipment. Students can call up lessons and complete assignments and assessments at workstations. Lectures are delivered live once per year and recorded via Internet-streaming technology for students to access anywhere and anytime on the college's computer network. In addition to basic instruction in engineering fundamentals, advanced learning modules are designed to enhance students' abilities to work independently and in teams, and to think critically and analytically to solve practical manufacturing problems.

Completed in 2002 on the college's Green Bay campus, the Center is open six days a week to provide access for working adults who need to fit college into busy work and family schedules. In addition to serving more than five hundred students in associate degree, technical diploma, and apprenticeship programs, the Center also provides facilities for an articulated manufacturing engineering program offered onsite jointly with the University of Wisconsin–Stout. The associate degree portion of this articulated program, Manufacturing Engineering Technology, admitted its first group of students in fall 2008. UW–Stout began providing instruction at the technical college in the junior- and senior-level course work beginning fall 2010.

A major area employer, Rockwell Automation, was instrumental in assisting the college with the design and initial equipping of the facility. Since then, other area employers including the Paper Converting Machine Company, Georgia-Pacific, and Hart Design have partnered with the college to donate converting and packaging machines for student capstone experiences as well as miscellaneous instructional supplies. The Center also provides area employers with a venue for customized technical training for incumbent workers.

Health Education Center at Chippewa Valley Technical College.   This center represents a unique partnership between the college, a public institution, and a private university. The college provides a home to over 1,600 students enrolled in nursing and allied health programs at its Eau Claire and River Falls campuses. A majority of the students in the college's sixteen health programs are located in the Center. In addition to its educational programming, the Center is the home for the University of Wisconsin Health–Eau Claire Family Medicine Clinic, which is a training site for medical school graduates specializing in family practice, and a dental clinic that offers full-service dental care to low-income residents from a number of counties throughout Wisconsin.

The collaborative relationship between the college, the University of Wisconsin–Madison, and Marquette University is evident throughout the Center. Practitioners work together to educate health-care professionals in a multidisciplinary, interactive, real-life environment. Students, instructors, and practitioners are able to take advantage of the state-of-the-art equipment in the simulation laboratory, in the Dental Clinic, and in the radiography and sonography labs. Partners share in the use and maintenance of equipment that would otherwise be unaffordable individually, and they collaboratively share information and grant-writing initiatives. The onsite dental clinic is an educational and service center, housing the college's Dental Assistant and Dental Hygienist programs. The clinic provides opportunities for dental students from Marquette University and a resident sponsored by Delta Dental to work side-by-side with dentists, dental assistants, hygienists, and receptionists to further their education in an active training environment. The Dental Clinic has recorded over 125,000 patient visits since October 2004.

Instruction for the nursing and allied health programs includes traditional classroom and clinical experiences. In addition, in the Virtual Medical Center, a simulation laboratory that resembles a multi-room emergency department, students interact with a variety of medical simulators to perfect the skills required for their clinical practice. Using scenario-based or individualized instruction, students are able to experience common, critical, and even rare clinical situations in a safe and controlled environment. This training requires students to work in teams and develop the critical and analytical thinking they will need to succeed in their professions.

Emergency Operations Center at Lakeshore Technical College. This center in Cleveland, Wisconsin, provides a real-life central command-and-control facility capable of carrying out the principles of emergency preparedness and emergency management or of disaster management functions at a strategic level in a simulated emergency situation. This state-of-the-art facility uses a wide variety of technologies to provide real-world experience to the Public Safety Division students in the emergency management, criminal justice and law enforcement, emergency medical services, and fire associate degree programs. Because an emergency operations center is responsible for the strategic overview of the disaster, center staff is expected to make operational decisions during an incident. In the Center's simulation format, students learn the common functions of all emergency operations centers and practice collecting, gathering, and analyzing data and making decisions that will potentially protect life and property. Training opportunities available through the Center focus on building teams of individuals who can assume responsibility for life or death situations, and developing strong communication, interpersonal, analytical, and problem-solving capabilities of individual team members.

These emergency operations centers, originally created as part of the U.S. civil defense, can be found in many nations and at all government levels, as well as in larger organizations that deal with large equipment or large numbers of employees, such as a fire department or health-care organization. In corporations and smaller jurisdictions, the center may be co-located in the same room as an emergency communications center. Because the Emergency Operations Center is a fully functioning facility, the college also has entered into agreements with local municipalities for use of the center in the event their facilities are damaged or made inoperable.

Wood Manufacturing Center of Excellence at Northcentral Technical College. This center represents a unique collaboration with county government and area employers to meet the need for a more highly skilled workforce to replace retiring workers and support advancing technology in the wood manufacturing industry of north-central Wisconsin. In 2006, local employers approached the college with a request to increase the availability of specialized training unavailable from other providers. The college worked with Langlade County's economic development committee to launch an effort with county and state officials to implement construction of a new educational facility. In September 2008, the Langlade County Board approved borrowing for the construction of a 30,000-square-foot wood technology economic development building on the college's Antigo, Wisconsin, campus. Langlade County will donate the Center to the college upon repayment of its ten-year loan. This gift will permit the college to provide state-of-the-art training for the wood- and forest-products industry throughout the county and showcase Langlade County wood products, supporting regional economic development efforts through enhanced governmental, industrial, and educational partnerships.

Initially, the Center will offer a technical diploma program in wood manufacturing technologies and an applied associate degree program in wood processes technologies. Once the Center is successfully established, the college will continue to research and incorporate into the Center's offerings of sustainable timber harvest, primary wood manufacturing, reconstituted wood products production, and bio-fuels programs. Students will be able to access all classes offered at the Center through instructor-led onsite instruction, streaming video Web conferencing, or online instruction.

In keeping with the instructional needs expressed by the business community, the wood processes technologies program offered at the Center will include instruction drawn from engineering, business, and forestry disciplines to develop skills and specialized knowledge required for the manufacturing, marketing, distribution, and end use of wood products. Curriculum for the program emphasizes innovative approaches for obtaining, manufacturing, using, and recycling wood and other sustainable products in an environmentally safe manner. In common with the other examples presented here, the Center emphasizes the importance in postsecondary career and technical education of integrating technical skill development with analytical, cognitive, and interpersonal skills. A capstone course in the wood processes technologies program, for example, will require teams of students to demonstrate their ability to solve design problems using the skills, knowledge, and abilities learned in earlier classes. As part of the course, teams of students will identify a design problem, research solutions, design a product, use machinery and equipment available in the Center to solve the problem, establish a budget for building a prototype, and then build an actual proof-of-concept prototype.

Working with other educational partners in the area, the college is creating an educational pathway in wood technologies that begins with a youth apprenticeship program at the secondary level offering high school students related instruction and on-the-job training with area employers. Upon high school graduation, these students may enter the related applied associate degree program at an advanced level and ultimately may choose to pursue an articulated baccalaureate program at the University of Wisconsin–Steven Point. These educational and career-laddering opportunities to be offered through the Center will provide students and employers with a wide range of training choices to meet their immediate and long-range goals. In addition, the Center will provide customized training, technical assistance, and continuing education to incumbent workers to help employers in the region remain competitive and ensure they have the workforce needed to implement technological and business process innovations.

Conclusion

Despite ongoing massive job losses and concerns about the impacts of automation in reducing skill needs in the workforce, new technologies such as computerization and information processing have transformed the U.S. workplace over the past forty years, expanding employment and rewarding workers who possess strong analytical, interpersonal, and complex communication skills. The multiple impacts of these new technologies in the workplace on community and technical colleges have increased the need for college programming to be responsive to the needs of employers and their community to ensure that the current and future workforce has the skills required to succeed in the workplace. The adoption of these new technologies has also changed both what needs to be taught and how colleges are delivering postsecondary career and technical education.

At the postsecondary level, career and technical education prepares individuals to enter specific industry-defined careers that enable them to live, learn, and work as productive citizens in a global society. It also provides opportunities for incumbent workers to upgrade their skills to retain employment in their current field or enter a new career. At its best, career and technical education does not just impart techniques for accomplishing specific tasks needed for a particular job, but also helps students and workers develop their abilities to work collaboratively, analyze and solve problems, and think critically—the kinds of skills, knowledge, and abilities valued in the workplace and that provide the foundation for future learning experiences.

The new models used by Wisconsin's technical colleges for anticipating future programming needs and developing appropriate program content and strategies for the delivery of postsecondary career and technical education emphasize the importance in the two-year college setting of building strong ties within the community with employers and other educators and can help provide examples for others in responding to these same needs. Specifically, two-year college leaders and practitioners might:

- Expand the venues and opportunities to communicate with employers and employees about emerging employment and skill needs on a regional or state level. Expanded use of program advisory committees, conducting targeted industry skill studies, conducting economic summits, and similar events are recommended.
- Create ongoing, formal and informal opportunities to bring area employers, policymakers, secondary and other postsecondary educators, and other stakeholder groups to campus to view facilities, talk with instructors and students, and build support for programs.
- Work closely with key stakeholders to identify how college programs can align with and strengthen other educational, economic development, and social service innovation efforts.

Looking beyond the Midwest, each region will have a unique and continuously changing pattern of technology adoption needs and priorities depending on the mix of business and industry sectors being served. In the twenty-first-century economy, the regional capacity of two-year colleges to identify and build instructional programs addressing next-generation technologies has never been more important to regional economic productivity, as well as to positive educational outcomes for individuals and institutions.

References

Handel, M. J. *Worker Skills and Job Requirements: Is There a Mismatch?* Washington, D.C.: Economic Policy Institute, 2005.

Jacobs K. J., and Dougherty, K. J. "The Uncertain Future of the Community College Work Development Mission: Community College Missions in the Twenty-First Century." *New Directions for Community Colleges*, no. 136. San Francisco: Jossey-Bass, 2006.

Manufacturing Skill Standards Council. "Certifying the Industrial Athlete of the Future." 2009. Retrieved March 1, 2011, from http://www.msscusa.org/index.htm

Partnership for 21st Century Skills (Home). "Partnership for 21st Century Skills: Framework for 21st Century Learning." 2004. Retrieved April 11, 2009, from http://www.p21.org/index.php?option=com_content&task=view&id=254&Itemid=120)

U.S. Bureau of Labor Statistics. *Computer and Internet Use at Work in 2003.* Economic News Release. U.S. Department of Labor, August 2005.

U.S. Department of Labor. *Futurework: Trends and Challenges for Work in the 21st Century.* Washington, D.C.: U.S. Government Printing Office, 1999.

JANET L. WASHBON was associate vice president of Policy and Government Relations for the Wisconsin Technical College System until August 2009. Currently she is a senior Scientist at the Wisconsin Center for Education Research at University of Wisconsin–Madison.

The Joyce Foundation's Shifting Gears initiative was launched in 2007 with the goal of increasing the number of workers in six Midwestern states who earn credentials that are valued by employers in their local labor markets. This chapter summarizes the policies adopted by Illinois and Wisconsin to support the implementation of career pathways and bridge programs to both improve the employment opportunities of low-skilled, low-income adults and enhance the competitiveness of the regional workforce.

Leveraging Workforce Development and Postsecondary Education for Low-Skilled, Low-Income Workers: Lessons from the Shifting Gears Initiative

Debra Bragg, Laura Dresser, Whitney Smith

Introduction

Shifting Gears was launched in 2007 by the Joyce Foundation, a Chicago-based organization focused on improving the quality of life of citizens residing in the Great Lakes region of the United States. The primary goal of Shifting Gears is to increase the number of low-skilled, low-income Midwestern adults who obtain college-level occupational credentials that have value in the labor market. This chapter presents the goals of the Shifting Gears initiative and the policy initiatives adopted by Illinois and Wisconsin. Drawing from research supported by each state (Bragg, Harmon, Kirby, and Kim, 2009; Valentine and Pagac, 2009), this chapter presents goals, strategic approaches, and lessons for practitioners who have responsibility for leading other regional workforce initiatives in the United States.

NEW DIRECTIONS FOR COMMUNITY COLLEGES, no. 157, Spring 2012 © 2012 Wiley Periodicals, Inc.
Published online in Wiley Online Library (wileyonlinelibrary.com) • DOI: 10.1002/cc.20006

The Shifting Gears Initiative

The Shifting Gears Initiative of the Joyce Foundation recognizes that postsecondary education that leads to industry-valued credentials can be a route to family-wage employment for millions of adult workers in the Midwest who are unemployed or underemployed. Duderstadt notes the importance of this strategy, observing that "low-skill (e.g., without college degrees), middle-aged, and older workers make up the fastest growing share of [the Midwestern] states' total population and available workforce, and constitute a larger share of Midwest state population than in the United States as a whole" (2011, p. 33). He and other researchers and policy analysts (see, for example, Austin and Affolter-Caine, 2008) contend that postsecondary education is a gateway to good jobs for low-skilled adults and imperative for strengthening the economic competitiveness of the Great Lakes region.

The theory of change that undergirds Shifting Gears purports that strategic funding and technical assistance can accelerate state policy that is necessary to bring promising programs for low-skilled, low-income adults to scale (Taylor, 2009). By supporting Midwestern states that are attempting to catalyze policy reform, specifically Illinois, Indiana, Michigan, Minnesota, Ohio, and Wisconsin, the Joyce Foundation has targeted critical resources (fiscal and human) to better educate low-skilled, low-income workers in the region. Price and Roberts (2009) summarize the four core strategies of Shifting Gears as follows:

1. *Policy change* to leverage improvements in systems and institutional practice
2. *Data utilization* to measure and foster improvements in policy and practice
3. *Stakeholder engagement* to generate ideas and buy-in for systems and institutional change
4. *Strategic communications* to cultivate stakeholder support for systems and institutional change

In several Midwestern states involved in Shifting Gears, career pathways and bridge programs are central to policy change to better link education, training, and support services so that adult learners, many of whom are members of groups historically underrepresented and underserved in postsecondary education, can enter into and progress through college and transition into employment. Bridge programs focus on the foundational competencies that adults need to enter into college, and they often explicitly link adult basic education (ABE) or developmental or remedial education and English-language learning (ELL) instruction with postsecondary education. Career pathways provide sequential curriculum and instruction that enable students to progress from one level of education to the next, offering industry-recognized credentials at critical milestones (Spence, 2007; Foster,

Strawn, and Duke-Benfield, 2011) that lead to the associate or baccalaureate degree. Many bridges and pathways contextualize teaching and learning by integrating basic skills and occupational content, and they supplement this applied instruction with student support services. Ultimately, these initiatives seek to improve students' career options and earning potential by providing a roadmap to demystify the postsecondary education and workforce systems that seem confusing and impenetrable to students.

To support Shifting Gears implementation, the Joyce Foundation assembled a team of experts who provide technical assistance to help states formulate a plan to support policy change. Data analysis and reporting is another area of technical assistance, including helping states to build the capacity to track how many low-skilled, low-income adults are receiving education and advancing into the labor market. Capacity building related to data is critical to improving system performance and drawing attention to the unique needs, trajectories, and issues facing low-wage adults. A third area of technical assistance focuses on bringing professionals from the six states together to share their plans and collectively consider difficult problems. Cross-site meetings and webinars are another vehicle to support professional development. The fourth area of technical assistance is strategic communications to elevate two ideas to a broad audience: the importance of investing in the education of low-skilled adults and the importance of using state policy to advance this agenda.

Shifting Gears in Illinois

To initiate Illinois' Shifting Gears initiative, community colleges were identified to lead the development and implementation of bridge programs. The Illinois Community College Board (ICCB) is the fiscal agent for federal adult education funding that is associated with Title II of the Workforce Investment Act (WIA), called the Adult Education and Family Literacy Act. K-through-12, community colleges, and community-based organizations are eligible to receive federal funds, but the ICCB and the Illinois Community College System are central to the state's leadership strategy. Building on this structure, the ICCB used a competitive process to select ten community colleges geographically distributed throughout the state to implement Shifting Gears. These sites included three colleges that are part of the City Colleges of Chicago and seven other community colleges located in the Chicago metropolitan area as well as the central and southern regions of the state. Each college developed bridge programs in health science, manufacturing, or transportation, distribution, and logistics (TDL), with most projects focusing on health science.

Two types of bridge programs were implemented in Illinois. *Model A, Developmental Education Bridge* (Model A–Dev Ed), sought to move students from development education to college-level course work, and *Model B, Adult Education Bridge* (Model B–Adult Ed), sought to transition students from adult education to postsecondary education, including offering instruction for English-language learners (ELLs). Model A–Dev Ed was implemented by three sites, and Model B–Adult Ed was implemented by seven. Regardless of the model, the initial recruitment plans of most sites called for attracting students who tested on the Test for Adult Basic Education (TABE) at the Adult Secondary Education (ASE) level, which is equivalent to grades 9 to 12; only a few sought students at the Adult Basic Education (ABE) level, which is equivalent to grades 6 to 8.9. However, as recruitment proceeded, some sites that did not initially pursue ABE students opened recruitment to these students to try to address their education and employment needs and test whether the bridge model could have broader appeal and impact. As the recession deepened in 2008, the leaders of several bridges became convinced that their programs could serve adults with literacy skills below ASE. These local leaders adjusted their bridge programs for students having lower literacy levels and actively recruited them, in part to help address local unemployment.

Illinois' Shifting Gears Evaluation

Evaluation of Phase One of Shifting Gears addressed the following questions:

- How were bridge courses and programs developed and implemented?
- What were the experiences and perceptions of key stakeholders, including students, of bridge programs and courses?
- What was the incidence of bridge course and program enrollment and completion?
- What was the impact of bridge courses and programs on students' transition to postsecondary education and employment?

Quantitative and qualitative data were collected during the 2008 calendar year, with most community colleges operating a pilot bridge program in spring 2008 and repeating the programs in fall 2008. Qualitative data were also collected in spring 2009 when several sites offered another bridge program and the state moved forward to scale up policy and program implementation (Bragg, Harmon, Kirby, and Kim, 2009).

Program Results.   Evaluation results pertaining to bridge program implementation produced several valuable findings:

Bridge Programs Offer Instructional Innovations.   Illinois' bridge programs offer a range of instructional innovations to meet the needs of low-skilled, low-income adults. These strategies include team teaching; computerized and online instructional supports; hands-on and laboratory-based instruction, including field trips; cohorts and other strategies to build community among learners; and various forms of active learning.

Curriculum Emphasizes Contextualized Instruction.   The notion of contextualization, referring to basic skills (math, reading, and writing), was observed in most sites, leading the state to adopt a definition of bridge programming that places contextualized learning as one of three core requirements, with the others being transition services and career development. In the case of the Shifting Gears initiative, contextualization referred to the integration of occupational vocabulary and career-related tasks and problems into basic skills instruction, which was prominent in sites implementing Model B–Adult Ed, and the integration of basic skills to supplement and reinforce basic skills aligned with occupational content, which was prominent in Model A–Dev Ed sites.

College Leadership Matters.   In sites where community college leaders (e.g., top- and mid-level administrators) embraced the bridge program concept, the evaluation found greater alignment of functional units and resources to support programming for low-skill adults than in sites where community college leaders were less informed and involved. Partnerships among unit leaders within community colleges were crucial to both the development and the implementation of bridge programs, particularly bridges that extended to career pathways that link adult education students to developmental education and occupational education.

A Bridge Definition Policy Helps to Clarify Expectations.   All three elements of Illinois' bridge program definition (i.e., contextualized instruction, transition services, and career development) were evident in the bridge programs that were implemented at the local level. Prior to adoption of the definition, local providers in Illinois were implementing a wide range of programs that they were calling a bridge program, but some of the variation in approach was resolved once the state adopted and disseminated a common definition. The definition created greater understanding of bridge programs among practitioners in the field, and it legitimized and gave impetus to local implementation.

Use of Transition Supports Is Correlated with Student Success. Correlational analysis revealed that higher rates of use of transition coordinators and case managers by bridge students were related to higher rates of student completion of their bridge programs. Higher rates of use of transition services included the following: students receiving admissions and financial aid assistance at least once; students receiving advising at least once; students receiving transportation assistance at least once; and students meeting more frequently with an assigned transition coordinator or case manager.

Student Outcomes.   The evaluation results also revealed differences between student outcomes associated with Model A–Dev Ed and Model B–Adult Ed. First, students who enrolled in Model A–Dev Ed bridges accessed transition coordinators and various student services more frequently than students enrolled in Model B–Adult Ed. This difference may be related to the close proximity and historic connections between the community colleges' developmental education units and the support service units. Developmental education is a recognized mission of community colleges in Illinois. Model A–Dev Ed students may have more access to and familiarity with student services than students participating in Model B–Adult Ed.

For Model B–Adult Ed, relationships with college units were not as formal or longstanding as with Model A–Dev Ed. In fact, the connections between the Adult Ed bridges and college-credit programs were sometimes very weak, with some colleges being unable to overcome these gaps during the first offering of their bridge programs. A contributing factor seemed to be that many Adult Ed instructors are part-time employees who have limited familiarity with the community college and limited professional connections to other college faculty and employees. Though disconnects remained evident, the evaluation results show some Adult Ed programs made progress in strengthening their connections to community college–credit units, especially occupational education.

Quantitative results also show nearly half of all students completed bridge programs, with a higher rate of completion (72 percent) for students enrolled in Model A–Dev Ed bridges than Model-Adult Ed bridges (42.1 percent). Nearly one-third of Dev Ed students continued to enroll in post-secondary education immediately after completing the bridge, with about one-quarter of these students enrolling in Dev Ed. By contrast, almost 15 percent of Adult Ed students continued to postsecondary enrollment, with 42 percent of these taking Dev Ed courses. Over 65 percent of the Dev Ed and over 50 percent of the Adult Ed students who entered and completed bridge programs were employed in low-wage jobs.

New Models.   Whereas the focus of phase one of Shifting Gears in Illinois was on Model A–Dev Ed and Model B–Adult Ed, new models emerged as the sites implemented attempted to address the needs of their particular students:

- **The English-as-Second-Language (ESL) Model.** Two community colleges customized and contextualized the Model B–Adult Ed to meet ESL students' needs in the occupational fields of manufacturing and TDL, including paying special attention to linguistic, cultural, social, and gender issues.
- **The Incumbent Worker Training Model.** One community college drew upon an existing relationship with a local health-care provider to offer Model A–Dev Ed contextualized instruction and customized transition services in licensed practical nursing (LPN). The company's decision to pay tuition up front and consider the bridge program in making future decisions about job promotions was important to students' decisions to participate.
- **The Hybrid Model.** A few community colleges blurred elements of Model A–Dev Ed and Model B–Adult Ed, creating a hybrid model. In one particularly interesting case, a community college engaged faculty from

the three functional areas of adult education, developmental education, and occupational education in program planning and development, and the shared experience of these faculty convinced them that a hybrid model would both benefit students and enhance the sustainability of their bridge programs. Recognizing that students who need basic skills instruction come from diverse backgrounds and can enter community colleges through multiple doors, this model helps students find the most suitable education and employment option for them.

Overcoming Barriers.   Two types of barriers were consistent impediments to implementation of bridge programs, and these barriers emerged regardless of whether Model A–Dev Ed or Model B–Adult Ed was implemented:

- **Organizational barriers.** The community college environment presented several challenges to bridge implementation, including the use of college placement exams that do not pinpoint students' basic skills competency gaps; limited student support services to address the types of personal challenges of low-skill, low-income adults; and limited administrative, curricular, and instructional structures to accommodate bridge program implementation.
- **Policy barriers.** The misalignment of systems, funding streams, and policy and program requirements associated with WIA Title I and Title II, the Carl D. Perkins IV legislation on Career and Technical Education (CTE), and institutional developmental education impeded bridge program implementation. Included in this group of barriers is a concern about low-skill adults' eligibility for WIA Title I funding and issues with co-mingling federal funding streams.

Changes in policy and practice to address these barriers included enhanced support services; concerted efforts to align adult education, developmental education, and occupational education; improved course approval procedures to facilitate fast-paced program development and delivery; and enhanced communication and coordination between departments internal to community colleges and between the local colleges and the state.

Shifting Gears in Wisconsin

The Wisconsin Department of Workforce Development and the Wisconsin Technical College System, with funding from the Joyce Foundation and in partnership with Workforce Development Boards, the Center on Wisconsin Strategy, and others, have engaged in a multiyear system reform effort designed to institutionalize career pathways and bridges across the state's adult education and training systems. The effort is named Regional Industry

Skills Education (RISE), and it seeks to support an array of career pathways and bridge programs with the following benefits for specific target audiences:

- *For low–income adults:* higher skills and better jobs through more accessible and navigable training and career-advancement systems
- *For employers:* a reliable supply of workers whose skills are geared to industry needs
- *For workforce training and education:* more effective engagement with industry and more efficient alignment of resources

Starting in 2007, Wisconsin began to make a convincing, evidence-based case to the state to establish career pathways and related bridge programs. The strategies for meeting employer skill needs and worker career advancement needs include:

- Policies and processes at the state and regional level that support career pathways and enable low-skilled, low-income workers to participate in them
- Replicable career pathways in key industry sectors
- Bridge programs in several areas of the state to streamline adult learner transition from basic skills to career pathways and to support the students' exploration, preparation, and engagement in occupational education

Career pathways associated with RISE offer low-income adults clear and reliable courses of action for building skills to progress in their careers. Figure 1 provides a graphic representation of the career pathways model associated with Wisconsin's RISE initiative.

Bridge instructional programming is the first step on the career pathway for adults with basic skills or ELL needs. To support low-income workers in bridge programs and career pathway learning, employers, workforce development agencies, educational institutions, and other community organizations collaborate actively to provide training resources and wraparound support services to the learner as well as to reinforce the value of continuing along the career pathway.

Projected Outcomes.   The RISE initiative has articulated the following intended outcomes:

- Higher number of low-income working adults enroll in postsecondary education
- Higher proportion of low-income working adults attain degrees, technical diplomas, or certificates
- Higher proportion of ABE, ELL, and developmental and remedial adult learners make a transition to and complete associate degrees, technical diplomas, or certificates
- Higher earnings and job quality for low-income adults engaged in career pathway

NEW DIRECTIONS FOR COMMUNITY COLLEGES • DOI: 10.1002/cc

Figure 1. Career Pathways Associated with RISE

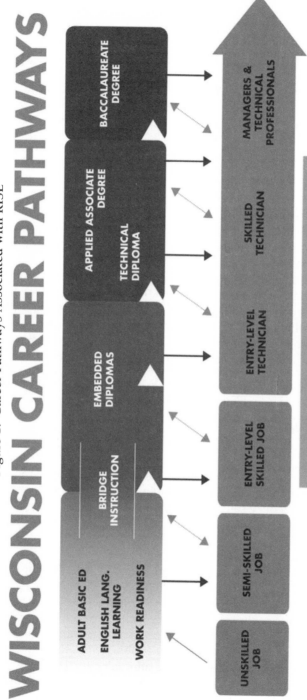

To achieve these outcomes and move Wisconsin's low-income workers through more successful postsecondary transitions and into family-sustaining jobs, RISE seeks fundamental system reform, first establishing a set of comprehensive guidelines for pathways and bridges, and then developing integrated policy, data, and communications action plans to support their development.

Career Pathway Guidelines.   Before embarking on a policy action agenda aimed at system reform, the RISE Steering Committee devoted time and energy to establishing a set of guidelines for workforce policymakers and practitioners. These guidelines, which became the initiative's foundational document, codified key elements of career pathways, including:

- Competency-based curricula tied to employer needs and industry skill standards
- Modular, sequential courses offering manageable steppingstones of skill-building, with relevant chunks tied to industry-recognized credentials
- Flexible course formats convenient for both working learners and employers
- Easy course credit portability for seamless progression through curricula supported by multiple institutions
- Roadmaps and other navigation aids showing connections between education, skill progression, and career opportunities
- Bridge programs preparing lower-skilled workers for postsecondary training toward credentials aligned with job advancement

A common definition provides Wisconsin with a foundation from which to build bridges and pathways.

Policy Priorities

- **Institutionalize pathways and bridges.** Ensure that career pathways, including bridge courses for ABE students and ELLs, become standard education and training options by revising program approval, classification, and funding policies. Specific institutional action steps delineated under three policy categories are: (1) eliminating or mitigating barriers to career pathway development, (2) aligning and developing funding sources, and (3) ensuring that the value of career pathways is recognized across education and workforce development sectors.
- **Refocus on human capital and support its development.** Shift Wisconsin's workforce development focus from immediate job placement to advancement through career pathways; institutionalize this effort through policies that improve assessment, career and benefits counseling, and referral; and make career pathway education and training more affordable for low-income working adults. Action steps are specified by (1) making career pathways more affordable for low-income working adults by increasing federal, state, and employer investment in related training; and (2) making career pathways a logical and accessible choice

for Wisconsin workers and job-seekers through policies that improve assessment, career and benefits counseling, and referrals.

• **Connect to industry partnerships.** Require state policies to improve employer engagement in key industries and integrate the work of RISE with related efforts to advance sector strategies in Wisconsin. Adopting a strong emphasis on employer engagement from the beginning, RISE recognized that a career pathway built without a deep understanding of and connection to a robust local industry is no more than an exercise in educational reform. Therefore, key stakeholders steered the project to deeper and more fundamental collaboration with Wisconsin industry partnerships.

Promising Results.   Wisconsin's first data project was a statistical profile of the RISE target population (the more than 700,000 low-wage working adults in Wisconsin who have no two- or four-year college credential or speak English "not well" or "not at all") and key occupational opportunities, including those with more than fifty average openings per year, paying more than a poverty-level wage, and requiring less than a four-year college degree. This work prompted the focused development of bridge and pathway programs on multiple levels. These data were also used to advance general policy for more and better postsecondary transitions, but the larger goal of the data project was to improve the measurement and reporting of key transitions and outcomes for adults accessing technical college services. Specifically, Wisconsin sought to (1) improve tracking and measurement of performance data for ABE, ASE, ELL, developmental, remedial, and postsecondary students and programming, and (2) strengthen Wisconsin's data and reporting system for technical college completion rates and employment and income effects. An ensuing pipeline study, now in its second iteration, includes data tables that show transitions for two age groups (eighteen to twenty-four and twenty-five to fifty-four), a set of tables comparing full- and part-time students, and considering transition from the lowest level of skill development through degree attainment. The report also shows these data for each Wisconsin Technical College System (WTCS) district. These state data tell a familiar but critically important story:

• Few ABE students enroll in postsecondary course work or postsecondary programs, although more than is the case in most other U.S. states.
• Many ABE students are able to succeed in college work, and ABE is good preparation. ABE students who enroll in postsecondary course work and programs perform well in comparison to students who start at the postsecondary level.
• ELL students enroll in postsecondary education at very low rates, but like ABE students, the ones who get to the postsecondary level do relatively well.
• Developmental and remedial education works in that students who participate do better than students who don't; however, relatively few students make effective use of this kind of preparation.

• Adult learners who enroll directly in college-level work often struggle. They do not accumulate college credits and earn credentials at the rate they could if they were better prepared.

These data suggest the WTCS and its partners can help low-skill students do better, and the colleges need to find ways to get more students into the programs of study and determine how they can be improved upon. Career pathways and bridges and policy reform to support their development will therefore continue to be a priority in Wisconsin.

Lessons Learned

Policy leaders in Illinois and Wisconsin have employed strategies that are uniquely important to their citizens, and they have capitalized on assets of their states and the Great Lakes region. The support of the Joyce Foundation, federal stimulus dollars, and other fiscal resources were employed to help implement career pathway and bridge programs for low-skill adults. In both states, Shifting Gears has led to new policy and incentives to link education and training efforts to better prepare low-skill, low-income adults for employment that can produce family-sustaining wages and address local unemployment during the Great Recession. Each state is tying its investments in new policy and program approaches to growing sectors of the Midwestern economy, ultimately "driving supply and demand closer" (Smith, cited in Taylor, 2009, p. 1).

Both Illinois and Wisconsin have made a number of important strides to serve low-skilled, low-income adults. Illinois has focused on increasing access to and success for adults who participate in adult education and developmental education bridge programs, recognizing that many adults need support to prepare for and enter college. Illinois' approach to Shifting Gears has focused on helping low-income adults gain the skills they need to get a foothold on postsecondary education and prepare for viable employment. The state's definition of a bridge program has been developed and disseminated widely to a broad range of stakeholders, including adult, developmental, and occupational education and other groups. To incentivize the development of more bridge programs statewide, Illinois is coordinating workforce and education policies that encourage more contextualized and applied instruction; additional support services; better alignment of federal funding streams within community colleges; and more fully integrated adult, developmental, and occupational education (Oertle, Kim, Taylor, Bragg, and Harmon, 2010).

Wisconsin identified career pathway and bridge programs as the intended outcome of its Shifting Gears initiative. The career pathways model was envisioned as a better way to deliver education services for low-income working adults because it is believed to facilitate more effective transitions from one level of education and skill development to another. Meeting local labor market needs is central to this approach, with the support of the state's workforce department and WTCS, which are collaborating to promote career pathways. In doing this work, Wisconsin recognized that new approaches to ABE and remedial education were needed, including new connections for students to technical college credit-based programs through bridge programs, as well as improved transitions within other credit-bearing programs toward two- and four-year degrees. Similar to Illinois' initiative, Wisconsin developed a definition of career pathways and bridge programs, and this definition has resulted in greater buy-in among practitioners and increased spread of desired practices. The *career pathway* definition is driving alignment within the state's systems by using funding guidelines and program approval processes that meet recommended standards.

Lessons for Practitioners

Looking beyond the Midwest, initiatives involving state governments, foundations, and community colleges offer some important insights for regional workforce development collaboration. Shifting Gears has taught state leaders and local practitioners the following:

- States can play a critical role in making the needs of low-skill, low-income adults known to policymakers and institutional leaders, and they can play a critical role in enhancing understanding of how to invest in this population.
- At the state and local levels, a broad-based group of state policymakers, practitioners, researchers, policy analysts, and employers agree on goals and action steps that can move a statewide agenda forward (Kirby, 2009). Developing clear and compelling descriptions of policies and program innovations helps to focus and mobilize implementation efforts that are aligned with state definitions and expectations.
- Research and evaluation is an important ingredient in state-level policy change associated with an initiative such as Shifting Gears. Without evidence that innovative programs are reaching the target population and improving student outcomes, it unlikely that states will sustain the changes long enough to bring about long-term systems reform.
- States agencies and local institutions need to align their goals and link their financial and operational systems in ways that enhance regional workforce and economic development. State and local collaboration has never been more important to achieve this goal.

References

Austin, J., and Affolter-Caine, B. "The Vital Center: A Federal-State Compact to Renew the Great Lakes Region." Washington, D.C.: Brookings Institution Metropolitan Policy Program, 2008.

Bragg, D. D., Harmon, T., Kirby, C., and Kim, S. "Initial Results of Illinois' Shifting Gears Pilot Demonstration Evaluation." Champaign, Ill.: Office of Community College Research and Leadership, University of Illinois at Urbana-Champaign, 2009. Retrieved from http://occrl.illinois.edu/files/Projects/shifting_gears/Report/SG_Eval _Report%20PRINT.pdf

Duderstadt, J. J. "A Master Plan for Higher Education in the Midwest: A Roadmap to the Future of the Nation's Heartland." Chicago, Ill.: Chicago Council on Global Affairs, 2011. Retrieved from http://www.thechicagocouncil.org/Userfiles/File/Globalmidwest /A_Master_Plan_for_Higher_Education_FINAL.pdf

Foster, M., Strawn, J., and Duke-Benfield, A. E. "Beyond Basic Skills: State Strategies to Connect Low-Skilled Students to an Employer-Valued Postsecondary Education." Washington, D.C.: Center for Postsecondary Education and Employment Success, CLASP, March 2011. Retrieved from http://www.clasp.org/admin/site/publications /files/Beyond-Basic-Skills-March-2011.pdf

Kirby, C. "Shifting Gears Phase Two: Advancing Policy." *Update on Research and Leadership*, Office of Community College Research and Leadership, 2009, 21(1). Retrieved from http://occrl.illinois.edu/Newsletter/2009/fall/1

Oertle, K., Kim, S., Taylor, J., Bragg, D., and Harmon, T. "Illinois Adult Education Bridge Evaluation: Technical Report." Champaign, Ill.: Office of Community College Research and Leadership, University of Illinois, October 2010. Retrieved from http:// occrl.illinois.edu/files/Projects/adult_bridge/Publications/AEBE_Report_FINAL.pdf

Price, D., and Roberts, B. "Educating Adult Workers: The Shifting Gears Approach to Systems Change." Chicago: The Joyce Foundation, December 2009.

Spence, C. "Career Pathways: A Strategy for Transforming America's Workforce Education Systems to Support Economic Growth." Denver, Colo.: Education Commission of the States, August 2007. Retrieved from http://www.workforcestrategy.org/images /pdfs/publications/ECS_CP_Paper_2007-08.pdf

Taylor, J. "Year Three of the Shifting Gears Initiative: An Interview with Whitney Smith from the Joyce Foundation." *Update on Research and Leadership*, Office of Community College Research and Leadership, 2009, 21(1). Retrieved from http://occrl.illinois .edu/Newsletter/2009/fall/1

Valentine, J., and Pagac, A. "Building Bridges in Wisconsin: Connecting Working Adults with College Credentials and Career Advancement." Madison, Wis.: Center on Workforce Strategy, University of Wisconsin–Madison, 2009. Retrieved from http://www .cows.org/pdf/rp-buildingbridges.pdf

DEBRA BRAGG *is a professor in the Department of Educational Organization and Leadership and director of the Office of Community College Research and Leadership at the University of Illinois–Urbana-Champaign.*

LAURA DRESSER *is associate director of the Center on Wisconsin Strategy at the University of Wisconsin–Madison.*

WHITNEY SMITH *is the employment program manager at the Joyce Foundation.*

6

This chapter defines innovation, explores how companies are reorganizing work and learning to promote innovation, and examines the implications for developing innovation talent in Midwestern high schools and two-year colleges.

Illinois Innovation Talent Project: Implications for Two-Year Institutions

Jason A. Tyszko, Robert G. Sheets

Introduction and Overview

There is a growing consensus that the United States and its regions, including the Midwest region, will increasingly compete on innovation (Council on Competiveness, 2005; IBM, 2006; Kao, 2007; Atkinson and Wial, 2008). This also is widely recognized in the business world (e.g., Chesbrough, 2006; Skarzynski and Gibson, 2008).

There is also growing consensus that innovation talent—the human talent to drive and support innovation—will be a major key. We will be able to compete on innovation only to the extent that we can develop and utilize innovation talent better than any other nation, region, and state in the world (e.g., Council on Competitiveness, 2005; Kao, 2007).

Despite this consensus, however, there is surprisingly little agreement on how we define innovation, and there is little agreement on what is needed to produce a new generation of innovation talent that can drive and support innovation in both the public and private sectors. Many early research and policy reports focused mainly on scientific and technological innovation and the need to prepare more scientists and engineers and a larger science,

---

This paper represents the views of the authors only and not necessarily the views of the Illinois Innovation Talent Project partners or the State of Illinois.

technology, engineering, and mathematics (STEM) focused workforce (e.g., National Academy of Sciences, 2007). However, this early focus did not fully capture the role of entrepreneurship and the growing importance of business-model innovation that is driving growth in many sectors (e.g., Chesbrough, 2006; IBM, 2006). It also did not capture the innovation work being done in the public and private sectors addressing large complex social, economic, and technological challenges (e.g., Kao, 2007).

The major challenge in the coming years will be developing a widely shared understanding of innovation and innovation talent and how we can best produce innovation talent throughout the P-20 educational pipeline, including two-year educational institutions. The Illinois Innovation Talent Project provides a useful example for exploring these questions. This chapter provides an overview of the Illinois Innovation Talent Project and the working definition of *innovation* used in the project and then explores implications for re-visioning the role of two-year colleges in producing innovation talent. The chapter first defines innovation, explores how companies are reorganizing work and learning to promote innovation, and then examines some of the implications for developing innovation talent. We then provide an overview of the Illinois Innovation Talent Project and its integration within a larger Illinois P-20 STEM initiative and conclude with implications for two-year educational institutions.

Defining Innovation and Challenges in Developing Innovation Talent

As outlined below, three challenges need must be addressed by leaders seeking to develop innovation talent in their local or regional workforces.

Defining *Innovation*.   Illinois launched the *Innovate Now* initiative in 2006 to raise awareness and explore the critical role of innovation in state and regional economic development. As part of that effort, Innovate Now reviewed research and policy reports and worked with leading experts to develop a working definition of innovation that could capture the full scope and complexity of innovation. In general, Innovate Now defines innovation as "the development and implementation of new ideas and new ways of doing things that create social value." When applied to the business world, the definition becomes more specific:

> Innovation is the development and implementation of new ideas and new ways of doing things to create customer value and drive business and economic growth. Innovation can occur in four spheres including business models, products and services, markets, and processes. Innovation includes both incremental improvements and breakthrough developments and is broader than science and technological discovery and advancement. It is the interface between entrepreneurship and science and technology discovery as well as other types of creativity and discovery. [InnovateNow, 2007]

This definition captures the full scope and complexity of the concept of innovation and shows the connections and interfaces of science and technology and entrepreneurship as well as of the fine arts and design. It also represents the full array of functions and academic disciplines. In addition it points to the interfaces between state and regional economic development efforts in entrepreneurship and science and technology development and transfer.

Innovation Talent: Growing Role of Open Cross-Functional, Interdisciplinary Teams. In order to compete on innovation, leading companies throughout the world are attempting to transform their internal cultures and structures to drive and support innovation at all levels of their organizations. They are moving management and research and development functions to front-line workers and engaging them in cross-functional, interdisciplinary teams with internal as well as external partners. They are asking all workers to be innovators. This is clearly seen in the following observation:

> In industry after industry, from computers to consumer goods to toys—all kinds of companies are waking up to the power of "connection and conversation" for driving new thinking and innovation. . . . What they are coming to realize is that everyone has the potential to be an innovator—to play a role in the creation of radical new ideas and exciting new solutions that could potentially influence the destiny of the company. [Skarzynski and Gibson, 2008]

The move to open cross-functional collaborative teams is being accelerated by the move to *open innovation* models and the use of leading innovation intermediaries (Chesbrough, 2006). It is also being accelerated through the expanded use of Internet-based crowd-sourcing strategies (Tapscott and Williams, 2006).

As found by the Council on Competitiveness (2005), the nature of innovation is changing rapidly by becoming more multidisciplinary and collaborative. Innovation increasingly occurs at the intersection of disciplines and functions, creating the "productive friction" (Hagel and Brown, 2005) essential to breakthrough and disruptive innovations. Also, as observed by the Council, innovation is becoming more "democratized," moving out of the domain of research and development departments and into open collaborative teams of front-line workers and customers working together with scientists, engineers, and business professionals. Finally, innovation is becoming more global with innovation originating from a diverse set of partners from all over the world engaged through leading-edge information technology tools.

Kao (2007) presents an even broader view of innovation, arguing that innovation will be driven by broader public–private collaborations that address the most fundamental challenges of our times in health care, energy, and overall environmental sustainability. By addressing solutions to these complex multifaceted problems we will drive both incremental and breakthrough innovations and spur economic growth.

These trends toward open collaborative innovation approaches are being supported by new innovation-focused economic development strategies that promote open collaborative networks at the state and local levels (Council on Competitiveness, 2005). These collaborative networks are designed to accelerate the pace of state and regional innovation by improving working relationships and synergies between public and private players within key clusters or sectors such as biomedicine and health care, energy, and transportation and logistics. These collaborative networks many times involve universities and colleges that play a variety of major roles.

Developing Innovation Talent in the P-20 Educational Pipeline. What are the implications of these trends in innovation and innovation-based economic development for developing innovation talent in the P-20 educational pipeline? It is clear from the innovation literature that students must have a new set of skills, especially new open collaborative problem-solving skills that make them capable of solving complex ill-structured real-world problems within cross-functional interdisciplinary teams. They also need stronger project-management and teamwork skills. Stronger global and cross-cultural orientations are assets that allow them to harness the talents and insights of a global set of partners from diverse backgrounds and experiences. Finally, they must be able to harness the power of information technology to reach out and connect and collaborate with project partners better and faster than competitors from throughout the world.

Developing this type of innovation talent will require major changes in high schools, colleges, and universities throughout the P-20 educational pipeline similar to what is being explored and pilot-tested in the Illinois Innovation Talent Project. This project is described in the following section.

Illinois Innovation Talent Project

Background. In 2008, Illinois was selected to participate in a National Governors Association (NGA) Policy Academy where leading state agencies, universities, and business associations came together and posed the question: What can we do to provide a more engaging and enriching learning experience for our students, one that will enable them to become more competitive learners and be better prepared to be innovators in our communities and workplaces? The Illinois team recommended launching an innovation talent initiative starting at the high school level. Since the NGA academy, an Advisory Board was established and includes the Illinois Governor's Office, the Illinois Department of Commerce and Economic Opportunity, the Illinois State Board of Education, the Illinois Mathematics and Science Academy, the Illinois Community College Board, the Illinois Board of Higher Education, the University of Illinois, iBIO and the iBIO Institute, the Chicagoland Chamber of Commerce, TechAmerica, Microsoft Corporation, and many others.

The Advisory Board was tasked with issuing recommendations on how to promote cross-functional critical thinking and project-management skills that reflect leading business models and prepare students to be innovators in the workplace and community. In addition, the Advisory Board was tasked with providing students with educational opportunities that are driven by problem-based learning experiences across disciplines that prepare students with the breadth and depth of knowledge to apply their skills in industry sectors such as health care, manufacturing, transportation and logistics, and financial services.

Innovation Talent is serving as one of our principal strategies for demonstrating the integration of the updated National Education Technology Standards (NETS). Our understanding of the updated NET Standards is that they envision the use of technology as a platform for innovation work through promoting open-collaborative networks that engage students as citizens, workers, and members of the community and have major implications in all major subject areas and applications of learning.

Pilot Phase Overview.   Based on the NGA Policy Academy Team recommendations, Jack Lavin, then-director of the Illinois Department of Commerce and Economic Opportunity, and Christopher Koch, superintendent of the Illinois State Board of Education, assembled a public–private partnership to work with Illinois high schools on a pilot initiative designed to promote innovation-centered education and to increase student achievement in math, science, and engineering. The objectives of the pilot phase were to:

- Demonstrate how the updated NET Standards can be used in an interdisciplinary curriculum that engages all levels of students in problem-based learning.
- Establish a pipeline of projects that continually engages Illinois schools and external partners, including business, government, and community entities.
- Provide students with career awareness through examining real-world problems from multiple disciplines and networking with outside professionals.
- Prepare educators to be able to establish connections with outside partners and develop curricula around problem-based learning.

Innovation Talent was launched during the 2008–2009 academic school year. As part of the pilot, twenty-nine schools across the state were connected with industry, government, and community partners to critically examine and solve complex problems as members of diverse interdisciplinary teams utilizing leading-edge information technology project management tools. The Illinois Mathematics and Science Academy (IMSA) played a key role in providing professional development and support to schools and their partners. These projects allowed students to connect and apply their learning in math, science, engineering, and social science by working as cross-functional interdisciplinary teams. As part of the pilot effort, community colleges and universities assisted with recruiting schools and, in some cases, provided professional support to the participating teachers as well as instructional assistance. The projects themselves were diverse and included challenges in the fields of information technology, health care, energy, manufacturing, logistics, "green" design, biotechnology, and many others (see Appendix A for a list of projects and partners).

Participants in the project had a wide range of experiences that captured the role of innovation. Joey, a participating student, explained that "this project helped us all to have open minds. It taught us that no idea is too crazy because it could spark a great idea. It also really made us think of how important it is to work together to accomplish our goals." On December 4, 2008, the *Daily Herald* (Chicago) ran an article on Rolling Meadows High School and the Illinois Department of Transportation (IDOT), the school's challenge sponsor. According to the *Daily Herald*,

> Using their knowledge of robotics and several high-tech tools, the students came up with a safe, efficient way to conduct bridge inspections that IDOT hadn't considered seriously in the past . . . they were quite impressed.

Strategies for Scalability.   The Innovation Talent Advisory Board recommended several key issues in making the program sustainable and scalable:

- *Endorsing the NET standards.* The Illinois State Board of Education is currently leading an effort to include the updated NET Standards as part of the Illinois Learning Standards review through the American Diploma Project—an effort to benchmark Illinois' standards and make college and career readiness a priority for students.
- *Teacher preparation and professional development.* Advisory Board members are working with problem-based learning experts specializing in math, science, and career and technical education, as well as schools of education, to organize forums designed to reach consensus on how to provide professional development and new teacher training to support problem-based learning.
- *Promoting innovation-centered learning environments.* In addition, we are having ongoing conversations with leading IT solution-based companies on addressing the implications of the NET Standards and how leading-edge information technologies will be incorporated into school infrastructure and classroom design. Recently, TechAmerica hosted a Twenty-First-Century Learning Environment symposium where public officials and leading IT specialists discussed the shift in challenges

from improving access to technology to what technology should be used for.

- *Facilitating school partnerships.* In partnership with IMSA and the University of Illinois at Urbana-Champaign, the State of Illinois has worked to develop an NSF Innovative Technology Experiences for Students and Teachers (ITEST) application to fund the development and implementation of a cyber-infrastructure that would allow partners to use the Web to post challenges to our community of schools and redefine how we understand the use of technology in teaching and connecting students to learning opportunities. Based on private-sector innovation models, this platform can be a single point of entry for companies to post challenges as well as provide virtual project management and networking space for students. In addition, this platform can be a portfolio-building resource that drives career guidance and can help connect students with a network of industry resources.

The lessons learned from Illinois Innovation Talent Project are now being imbedded as part of the State of Illinois' STEM education reforms envisioned as part of its Race to the Top application. The state is in the process of scaling up Programs of Study for all students where each student develops a personalized education plan aligned to their academic and career interest. Programs of Study are modeled after the National Career Cluster Framework, which organizes each industry cluster by career pathways. Work-based learning is now envisioned to be a core part of the delivery of a Program of Study's P-20 learning progression.

The Illinois Innovation Talent Project provides an example of how industry-sponsored problem-based learning can be used as a work-based learning experience in a P-20 Program of Study. Given that the state will be scaling up Programs of Study for all students and not just career and technical education students, the need for a wide range of work-based learning opportunities is necessary. The Illinois Innovation Talent project helps provide a means for building capacity where industry partners can now interface with interdisciplinary teams of students on a real-world project as opposed to working with a smaller number of students through more traditional work-based learning opportunities. The state is now exploring how to support matchmaking between student teams and industry partners using new learning management system tools that leverage cloud-computing technology.

Implications for Two-Year Institutions

As noted earlier, the first national reports on innovation focused on technological innovation and the role of scientists and engineers. They also focused on the need to expand research and development at major research universities and laboratories and private-sector research and development facilities throughout the country. This left many to think that there is only a limited role for two-year educational institutions in driving and supporting innovation other than developing more students to enter universities and pursue STEM-related fields.

However, as we have argued here, innovation is more than that. It is the development of new ideas and new ways of doing things at all levels of the organization, involving workers from all different cultural, social, and educational backgrounds and experiences. As a result, the development of innovation talent should be central to the mission of all educational institutions, including high schools, community and technical colleges, and universities. As we introduce students to problem-based learning challenges in secondary education, it is important to make sure that these students continue to develop their problem-solving and project-management skills as they continue their educational development at two-year institutions or universities. Two-year institutions are also part of an education network that can benefit from connecting with the larger community of problem-solvers. Cross-functional teams of community college students should compete to solve industry and government problems alongside students from other institutions, or partner with them as members of collaborative teams. For example, two-year institutions can play an important role in providing mentors and project leaders as they partner with secondary education students, thereby supporting curriculum and standards alignment. They can also be involved in joint projects with university students to further continue and extend curriculum and standards alignment.

What are the barriers for two-year educational institutions in playing a central role in developing innovation talent? We see four major barriers. These barriers exist at all postsecondary institutions, including universities.

First, two-year educational institutions, like their university counterparts, are organized around major disciplinary and program silos in which students are not given the necessary depth and breadth of learning and experiences needed to be effective in cross-functional interdisciplinary teams. In addition, students are usually given internships and other work-based learning experiences within their own programs and not through interdisciplinary cross-functional team projects involving students from other programs except through a limited number of capstone courses and special projects. Current educational institutions are organized around the same silos of functions and disciplines that were once the hallmark of leading companies from around the world. These silos are now being broken down as companies restructure to promote and support innovation. Like universities and high schools, two-year educational institutions must undergo the same organizational restructuring as American businesses to promote and support problem-centered interdisciplinary and cross-functional work and learning like their business counterparts have been doing over the past few years. They also must establish a new approach to work-based learning that gives students the opportunities to engage in real-world problem-solving projects similar to what is being done with the Illinois Innovation Talent Project with high school students.

The Illinois implementation of career clusters based on the national career clusters framework is a promising first step, because this framework emphasizes a proper balance between depth and breadth. When systematically implemented, career clusters provide students with depth of knowledge and skill in at least one occupational or program specialty, as well as sufficient breadth to apply that expertise to one or more sectors. Clusters provide an initial framework for students to work together on real-world problems that are interdisciplinary and require both breadth and depth of knowledge within industry sectors such as health care, manufacturing, transportation and logistics, financial services, and many others. However, these clusters must be implemented in ways that do not merely create larger silos but rather allow students to address complex problems that involve students from more than one cluster.

Second, two-year institutions, like their university counterparts, also must begin to break down the silos between two major functions—educating students and promoting community and economic development. They also must rethink their role in research and technology transfer in the context of a broader definition of innovation presented in this chapter. These two changes would allow two-year colleges to leverage greater synergies and resources for the benefit of their students, communities, and regions. For example, students could be engaged in innovation projects that further their education, promote technology transfer, contribute to community development, and help create and retain jobs in their communities all at the same time. Two-year educational institutions can play an important role in promoting innovation within collaborative networks in their regions in cooperation with universities and firms.

Third, two-year educational institutions, like other educational systems and institutions, must develop new information technology infrastructures that are modeled off business infrastructures that support innovation projects carried out by open cross-functional interdisciplinary teams. This will require a new approach that goes well beyond traditional online learning infrastructures and even new applications of information technology for personalized learning (e.g., Christensen and others, 2008). It will require developing a new platform for students to engage in real-world projects with external business, government, and nonprofit partners as well as other colleges and universities that are based on leading platforms and tools being used in workplaces (e.g., McAfee, 2009). These platforms and tools should be implemented across the entire P-20 system similar to what is being planned and developed as part of the Illinois Innovation Talent Project and the new learning and performance management system for the Illinois STEM initiative.

Fourth, two-year institutions, like their university partners, do not have the incentives to break down silos, utilize new infrastructures, and provide their students with complex challenging projects with external partners using new technology infrastructures. Future state and regional innovation and STEM initiatives must develop new strategies to incentivize and support two-year institutions in making these major changes.

Summary and Recommendations for Two-Year College Leaders

There is a growing consensus that the United States and each of its regions will increasingly compete on innovation. The key will be how we develop innovation talent better than any other country and region in the world. The major challenge over the coming years is in developing a widely shared understanding of innovation and identifying how we can best produce innovation talent throughout the P-20 educational pipeline, including two-year educational institutions. We have argued that innovation is more than scientific and technological research and development and involves the development and application of new ideas and new ways of doing things at all levels of organizations across the public and private sectors.

The development of innovation talent requires community and technical college leaders, regardless of regional context, to think and act differently. First, the world of innovation is changing rapidly and increasingly involves the work of cross-functional interdisciplinary teams from diverse educational backgrounds, including two-year degrees and certificates. Thus, two-year college leaders and their faculty members must play a more central role in developing innovation talent in cooperation with high schools and universities.

Second, the Illinois Innovation Talent Project's inclusion in Illinois' P-20 STEM initiative provides a useful example for exploring the re-visioning of the role of two-year college teaching and learning. Producing innovation talent through interdisciplinary instruction requires two-year institution leaders to address the four key barriers or challenges outlined earlier. When successfully addressed with solutions such as collaborative faculty development and new information technology infrastructure, innovation talent initiatives can be critical drivers for enhancing economic development at the community, regional, and national levels.

References

Atkinson, R., and Wial, H. *Boosting Productivity, Innovation, and Growth through a National Innovation Foundation.* Washington, D.C.: Brookings and Information Technology and Innovation Foundation, 2008.

Chesbrough, H. *Open Business Models: How to Thrive in the New Innovation Landscape.* Boston: Harvard Business School Press, 2006.

Christensen, C., Horn, M., and Johnson, C. *Disrupting Class: How Disruptive Innovation Will Change the Way the World Learns.* New York: McGraw-Hill, 2008.

Christensen, C., and Raynor, M. *The Innovator's Solution: Creating and Sustaining Successful Growth.* Boston: Harvard Business School Press, 2003.

Council on Competitiveness. *Measuring Regional Innovation: A Guidebook for Conducting Regional Innovation Assessments.* Washington, D.C.: Council on Competitiveness, 2005.

Hagel, J., and Brown, J. S. *The Only Sustainable Edge: Why Business Depends on Productive Friction and Dynamic Specialization.* Boston: Harvard Business School Press, 2005.

IBM. *Expanding the Innovation Horizon: The Global CEO Study.* Somers, N.Y.: IBM Corporation, Global Services, 2006.

Innovate Now. *Innovate Now: A Public/Private Initiative to Build a Sustainable Growth Economy in Illinois,* Chicago, IL: Chicagoland Chamber of Commerce, 2007.

Kao, J. *Innovation Nation: How America Is Losing Its Innovation Edge, Why It Matters, and What Can We Do to Get It Back.* New York: Free Press, 2007.

McAfee, A. *Enterprise 2.0: New Collaborative Tools for Your Organization's Toughest Challenges.* Boston: Harvard Business Press, 2009.

National Academy of Sciences. *Rising Above the Gathering Storm: Energizing and Employing America for a Brighter Economic Future.* Washington, D.C.: National Academy of Sciences, 2007.

Skarzynski, P., and Gibson, R. *Innovation to the Core: A Blueprint for Transforming the Way Your Company Innovates.* Boston: Harvard Business Press, 2008.

Tapscott, D., and Williams, A. *Wikinomics: How Mass Collaboration Changes Everything.* New York: Penguin Group, 2006.

JASON A. TYSZKO is a policy adviser for economic development in the Office of Governor Pat Quinn, State of Illinois.

ROBERT G. SHEETS is director of research and development in the Business Innovation Services unit at the University of Illinois at Urbana-Champaign and a policy adviser for the Illinois Department of Commerce and Economic Opportunity.

NEW DIRECTIONS FOR COMMUNITY COLLEGES • DOI: 10.1002/cc

Appendix A

Environmental and Tourism Problems		
School	Business/Organization Partner	PBL Topic
Alton High School	Great Rivers Land Trust	How does a new business opening, such as a Wal-Mart, impact water quality in the local watershed?
Astoria High School	Chautauqua Wildlife Refuge Illinois Department of Natural Resources	How can the Chautauqua Wildlife Refuge educate the public about the educational and recreational value of this resource?
Casey-Westfield High School	City of Casey Illinois Environmental Protection Agency	How might we develop a sustainable recycling program and inform both the school and community?
Christopher High School	Illinois Historical Preservation Agency Mulkeytown Area Historical Society Southern Illinois Tourism Bureau	How can we leverage the historical sites to generate tourism income and job opportunities for Mulkeytown and Christopher?
Hyde Park Academy	City of Chicago, Department of the Environment	How might we establish a recycling program that has a broader environmental significance?
O'Fallon Township High School	City of O'Fallon Illinois Environmental Protection Agency Trumpet Builders Wellspring Development Company	How might students design a house for a proposed sustainable development that is eco-friendly, cost effective, appealing, and marketable?

iBIO Problems		
School	Business/Organization Partner	PBL Topic
Chicago High School for Agricultural Sciences	Valent BioSciences Corporation	How might Valent BioSciences Corporation address the need for an environmentally compatible mosquito-control and public health information program?
Eisenhower High School	Tate & Lyle	How might we advise Tate & Lyle about future investment of staff time and research dollars in further development of bio-fuels?
Lindblom Math & Science Academy	Baxter International	How can we help Baxter's renal division increase the compliance rate of children on home dialysis?

iBIO Problems		
School	Business/Organization Partner	PBL Topic
MacArthur High School	Tate & Lyle	How might we improve efficiency of the Tate & Lyle processing of both GMO (genetically modified) and non-GMO corn products for different global markets?
Maine East High School	Astellas Pharma US	How might we advise Astellas about whether the pharmaceutical company should continue development of drugs to combat the superbug, Methicillin-resistant *Staphylococcus aureus,* commonly known as MRSA?
Niles West High School	Abbott Laboratories	How might Abbott advocate for personalized medicine in a way that positively impacts patient health and addresses the practical and ethical considerations raised by personalized medicine?

Transportation, Technology, and Health Problems		
School	Business/Organization Partner	PBL Topic
Glenbrook Academy of International Studies	Allstate Insurance	Are there better predictive factors besides just grades, age, and gender to set fairer auto insurance premiums?
Marine Military Academy	Argonne National Laboratory	What is the feasibility and practicality of Personal Air Vehicles?
Niles North High School	PCTel American Electronics Association	What inventory and tracking system might we design for our school's auto lab Netbook computers to ensure student accountability?
Senn High School New Athens High School	TEC Services Consulting Broadband Deployment Council American Electronics Association	What social networking prototype might address the needs of both students and school administrators? How can we advise the New Athens town council on developing a plan for creating wireless zones?

Continued

Transportation, Technology, and Health Problems

School	Business/Organization Partner	PBL Topic
Thornridge High School	NOW Foods	How might we design and pilot a standardized consumer test for NOW Foods' new product, Stevia, its healthy alternative sweetener?
Williams Preparatory School of Medicine	Illinois Department of Public Health, Office of Health Promotion	How might we prepare a health campaign encouraging preteens and teens to make healthy choices in the areas of nutrition, physical fitness, and tobacco use?

Energy Reduction Problems

School	Business/Organization Partner	PBL Topic
After School Matters	City of Chicago Chicago Public Schools	How might we reduce the waste produced in our school's kitchen and cafeteria?
William Fremd High School	Commonwealth Edison	How can we develop a prioritized plan for reducing the energy consumption in our school?
Genoa-Kingston High School	Commonwealth Edison SAERIS, a Division of Acuity Brands Lighting Custom Aluminum Products	How might we develop an optimal plan for reducing the energy consumption and costs in our district's five school buildings?
Manteno High School	Commonwealth Edison Village of Manteno	How might we reduce the energy usage in five public buildings in our community?
Reavis High School	Commonwealth Edison Reavis High School Maintenance Department	How can we reduce fuel consumption and costs of district vehicles and the air and noise pollution that accompanies internal combustion engines?
Thornton Township High School	Commonwealth Edison AbitibiBowater Recycling Division South Side Electric	How can we evaluate ways to reduce the energy costs of our school?
Waubonsie Valley High School	Commonwealth Edison	How can we enact change at our high school to reduce energy consumption and costs?

Industrial Problems

School	Business/Organization Partner	PBL Topic
Limestone Community High School	Excel Foundry & Machine	How might Excel Foundry redesign the head ball-and-socket liner combination in its rock crusher to reduce the current failure rates?
Rochelle Township High School	Nestlé USA	What effective inventory system might we design for Nestlé USA to track pallets from various vendors in their regional warehouse?
Rolling Meadows High School	Illinois Department of Transportation	Using robotics, how can inspections of the 8,000 bridges in Illinois be performed in a safe and cost-effective manner?
United Township High School	John Deere Harvester Works	What is the best design for a multipurpose portable device to move small utility vehicles onto any transport vehicles of various sizes and makes?

7

This chapter reviews the recent trends in general education and curricular innovations and profiles the role of general education in a forward-looking two-year Midwestern technical college program.

Learning to Innovate in Twenty-First-Century Community Colleges: Searching for the General Education Niche in Two-Year Colleges

Todd C. Lundberg

Over the past decade, policymakers have settled on a dominant narrative about the role of the community college in U.S. higher education. The story begins by establishing the importance of access to college. More education, the story goes, is related to greater personal and general stocks of economic, social, and human capital, as well as enhanced well-being (McClenney, 2004). The story culminates in a claim: if U.S. citizens are to compete successfully in a global economy, care for an aging population, deal with changes in the geopolitical and ecological context, and simply live well, then more citizens must have a higher education. The two-year college[1] plays a central role in this story, for it is at these colleges that most students will (re)learn technical knowledge and skills, thereby enhancing their capacity to add value to emerging industries, civic life, and their own personal development.

There are two implicit expectations about community college learning in this story. First, twenty-first-century learning involves both the mastery of industry-specific skills and knowledge as well as nuanced capacities to define problem spaces innovatively, compare phenomena critically, communicate in a wide variety of modes with a variety of technologies, and

New Directions for Community Colleges, no. 157, Spring 2012 © 2012 Wiley Periodicals, Inc.
Published online in Wiley Online Library (wileyonlinelibrary.com) • DOI: 10.1002/cc.20008

83

learn continuously (Gibbons and others, 1999; Bransford, Brown, and Cocking, 2000; Bragg, 2001; McClenney, 2004). Second, this learning will require approaches to learning and teaching that are radically different from those in place at most institutions. Students will develop "twenty-first-century skills" as Peter Drucker's *knowledge workers* or Robert Reich's *symbolic analysts* in part outside traditional courses and classrooms, in learning communities, service-learning experiences, and internships.

The chapters in *Advancing the Regional Role of Two-Year Colleges in the Twenty-First Century* imagine how community colleges in the upper Midwest might be restructured to meet the ambitious challenge put to community colleges nationally: to become engines of innovation that increase educational attainment and help citizens live well in global, knowledge-based societies. The authors describe institutions and initiatives that engage learners and colleges directly in the activity of (re)building the economic vibrancy of a region. This chapter seeks to fill a void in this important agenda by exploring the general education needed by newcomers to higher education that will enable them to contribute in multiple ways in the twenty-first-century workplace. There are good reasons for the omission: what students need to learn in the first year of college is diverse and determined locally; "general education programs," often seen as a fixed sequence of transferable courses, seem to lie outside the areas of innovation that matter. In an effort to become more precise about the kind of general education that Midwestern community colleges need to create, this chapter will approach two questions: In what ways is general education changing in response to the emerging educational demands of the twenty-first century? And, in what ways are Midwestern colleges engaging general education differently to develop twenty-first-century learners and citizens capable of invigorating their region? The chapter will review recent literature on general education trends and curricular innovations and profile the role of general education in a single, forward-looking two-year technical college program.

GE at the End of the Twentieth Century: Moving from Transfer to Learning

Discussions[2] of *general education* (GE) are predicated on an unstable distinction between liberal–general education and vocational or occupational education (Brint and Karabel, 1989; Pusser and Levin, 2009) and are haunted by contingent questions about what is an educated citizen.[3] These discussions cross the boundary between junior and senior colleges and increasingly draw in technical colleges. Across these institutions, the label *general* is persistent, though its meaning is neither precise nor consistent. In their systematic review of this "dynamic tradition," Conrad and Wyer (1980) argued that in the 1970s, GE curricula had been unable even in principle to resolve the tension between providing an educational opportu-

NEW DIRECTIONS FOR COMMUNITY COLLEGES • DOI: 10.1002/cc

nity to a diverse (and diversely prepared) student body and guiding all students to general intellectual and moral development. They inferred a set of trends—a continued commitment to a core of common classes, learning outcomes integrated into programs that often had professional ends, and emphases on process and development—and an inherited disconnection or opposition between liberal and occupational education. They also speculated that a pluralistic society might manage to integrate general and professional development through the ethical enterprise of inquiry. GE reforms since have wrestled with structure (i.e., which classes to require), learning outcomes (i.e., how to focus GE on interdisciplinary knowledge and inquiry skills), and purpose (i.e., how to articulate GE so as to help students and teachers see the relevance of GE learning to their worlds and goals).

The decade following the publication of Conrad and Wyer's *Liberal Education in Transition* saw a wave of GE reform that resulted in a more integrated and rigorous first-year experience. By 1993, an issue of *New Directions in Community Colleges* argued for a "second wave" of reform that might solve the thorny problem of community college GE through a more coherent and restrictive outcomes-based curriculum, through a curriculum focused on "habits of thought," through more inclusive college cultures, or through the infusion of GE into professional/technical courses. This curriculum would also integrate developmental education into the GE experience. The 1995 and 1999 volumes of *New Directions for Community Colleges*, in follow-up to the 1993 volume, were suggestive of the nature of ensuing GE reform in community colleges. The former offered case studies that demonstrated creative approaches to measuring general learning without making a break from the tradition. The latter reported on the 1998 findings from a twenty-three-year longitudinal study of the "undergraduate curriculum" conducted by the Center for the Study of Community Colleges (CSCC). The community college was in general praised for its responsiveness to students and local economies, but reform was limited to preserving core functions—transfer and non-transfer (i.e., remedial and occupational) courses—while expanding "non–liberal arts courses" as well as interdisciplinary courses and "multiculturalism courses." Reviewing the data on GE, the chapters in the 1999 volume of *New Directions* frequently celebrated the continued presence of a discernible, transferable liberal arts experience in community college curricula, though they worried about the extent to which students' habits of thought were challenged and developed by those curricula.

The CSCC study method, however, may be as revealing of GE reform as the findings from analyses of the study. The CSCC study reviewed catalogs, course schedules, and enrollment data, using data coding protocols based on those established in 1975, when Cohen initiated the study. For example, the study indicated the potential for interdisciplinary courses to connect general and occupational education, to cultivate learning communities, and to create an ethos of inquiry, but the data limited analysis to a count of kinds of courses offered by institutions represented in the study. The CSCC study verified that community colleges were meeting their diverse, inclusive missions of transfer, remediation, vocational education, and continuing education. But the chapters in this volume were unable to respond directly to persistent concerns about the adequacy and consistency of learning experiences at community colleges (Brint and Karabel, 1989). Moreover, the study did not address the nascent speculations about how the community college might evolve to meet changing demands made of higher education more broadly, nor did it address a series of concurrent calls for more direct measures of learning.

As the century ended, community college GE reform called for facilitating the development of the intellectual capacities needed in a changing social and cultural context, but GE programs focused on efficiently providing courses that transferred to four-year colleges. At this same moment, discussions at the four-year college began to shift from courses to learning. The GE 2000 and CAO 2000 surveys conducted through the Center for the Study of Higher Education described early attempts to design a more coherent, restrictive GE—one offering thematic and often topical courses aimed at teaching transferable skills and knowledge in place of entry-level courses within disparate disciplines. An emphasis on reviewing and ideally also assessing the capacities to be developed in a GE experience was first reported by Johnson, Ratcliff, and Gaff (2004). These trends would soon be well represented in the literature about GE in four-year colleges (University of California, 2007) and two-year colleges (Miles and Wilson, 2004). Still, while GE at the end of the century involved describing, documenting, and improving the kind of learning a generally educated citizen was able to do, community college GE continued to be defined in terms of the courses that citizens had to take to meet institutional requirements (Bragg, 2001). In some sense, GE programs continued to play the sorting role noted by Brint and Karabel (1989), convincing some students that transfer was for them, others that a terminal option might be preferable, and still others that they could take GE courses to help them decide why they were in college. These roles, of course, were increasingly dysfunctional since the once generally accepted community college definition of GE (i.e., GE includes those courses that transfer to a four-year college) had largely lost its ability to explain the role GE was coming to play (Cohen and Ignash, 1994).

General Learning in the Twenty-First Century: Considering Productive Inquiry

Over the past decade the aim and assessment of GE programs has increasingly included a consideration of students' learning on campus, while what counts as learning has begun to be defined off campus. Learning outcomes and related core learning experiences have been articulated and rearticulated. Credentials have been described in developmental terms, as movement toward a next phase of development, whether that next phase primarily had an academic focus (AAC&U, 2007) or a vocational one (Bragg, 2001). The notion that community colleges provide a *terminal* education had, since a 1994 review of the community college curriculum, been laid to rest: twenty-first-century GE has to be *transferable*, as learning if not as credit.

This new version of GE was driven by a set of assumptions shared by scholars from organizational learning, business, and public policy: workers and learners needed to be able to produce and adapt knowledge rather than primarily to master an existing tradition (Gibbons and others, 1999; Kress, 2003; Gee, 2004). Gibbons and others (1999) provided a detailed analysis of how these assumptions were changing higher education. Students needed to be prepared to learn and work in transdisciplinary, dynamic, informal, and applied settings on decentralized projects that linked highly specialized workers who produce unexpected and novel forms of knowledge. They needed to be able to see the production of knowledge in an ethical process and to measure success in terms of utility, profitability, and cost effectiveness and not only in terms of completeness or correctness. They needed not only to make use of communication and data sharing technologies but to feel at home in collaborative networks and using research skills. These learners needed to be prepared to produce results while they were learning new knowledge and skills. These basic assumptions found systematic expression in broad-based learning outcome initiatives as diverse as those of the League for Innovation in the Community College (the League), the AAC&U, and the Partnership for 21st-Century Skills (P-21). These separate projects argued that students need to develop skills in critical and integrative thinking, communication (including communication across cultures), the use of technology, problem solving, collaboration, innovation, and civic involvement, and to a lesser extent disciplinary and cultural knowledge. Most of these outcomes were raised in the GE 2000 survey.

Not surprisingly, few colleges have been organized in a way that enables them to make these or any set of learning outcomes central to GE. Organizing GE programs around consensus outcomes has been perceived, in some cases, to be subversive, even counterproductive for well-managed institutions; outcomes seemed to undermine traditional curricular and institutional structures, overload already limited capacities to collect and manage information about learning, and call attention to a lack of familiarity with and interest in membership in a learning college among learners and teachers. Calls like those in the 1998 Boyer Commission Report for making learning more central to GE provided few detailed strategies for overcoming these barriers.

GE as Three Sites for Productive Inquiry

What emerges from the past decade of GE reform is not the broad adoption of a set of twenty-first-century learning outcomes or a universal set of twenty-first-century curricular structures. Rather, the consensus in the literature seems to be a call for two-year colleges to establish and sustain three sites of knowledge production.

First, twenty-first-century GE programs are the construction of ongoing inquiry into the kinds of curricular structures that will support learning that is consistent with institutional values as well as with emerging modes of knowledge production and student needs. A twenty-first-century GE program could be implemented as a core of required discipline-specific courses, an integrated first-year experience, or a sequence of competence assessments. However, the program designers and implementers must make explicit the ways in which curriculum mediates student development as well as local, regional, and even global development. Additionally, the way in which the curriculum is reviewed and revised must be considered. Johnson, Ratcliff, and Gaff (2004) described some initial general strategies that a college might consider, but each college will make ongoing decisions about how GE curricular structures accomplish its mission.

Second, the next generation of GE programs must have the capacity to collect, analyze, and use information about student learning and success. Additionally, future programs will be grounded in data collection processes such as electronic portfolios or national databases of college effectiveness rather than distribution requirements.

Third, twenty-first-century GE programs provide learners, faculty, and institutions with public opportunities to reflect on and take responsibility for developing the capacities of individual students and their communities. There is increasing attention paid to the distinction between assessment—observation and analysis that enable judgment—and reflection—observation and analysis that enable understanding. Reflection is a critical aspect for the education of practitioners who seek to make learning transferable across contexts (Bransford and others, 2000). If institutions are to be sure that students have opportunities to acquire competencies that enable them to create value and innovate, they must have the capacity to reflect continuously on who their students are, who their students aspire to become, and what opportunities are open to those students.

Constructing programs around these three sites of inquiry will challenge the way that learners, teachers, institutions, and educational policy represent the purpose of GE in much the same way that cultivating the knowledge economy has challenged prior notions of research and development. In their often-cited *Change* essay, Barr and Tagg (1995) called on higher education to face this challenge in general ways fifteen years ago. Taking up that challenge fifteen years later in a 2009 policy paper for the Center for American Progress, Pusser and Levin began to suggest in more detail how community colleges might be "re-imagined." If community college students are prepared for "advanced learning and environments beyond the community college," the colleges have to reconceptualize their multiple functions as support for their students and then develop forms appropriate for those new functions. The re-imagined community college necessarily deconstructs "traditional typologies of community college student aspirations: vocational or transfer, in which students and programs are either oriented to the workplace or further education" (p. 13). At the same time, the community college no longer draws on a prominent theory-in-use defining community college students. A more functional understanding of students is rooted in four basic premises: students may not have clear intentions concerning their final goals; student talent does not have a static quality; students cannot adequately be understood in terms of abstract information; and students' needs for developmental education are central to the mission of the community college. In Pusser and Levin's student-centered community college, GE is neither an expression of the transfer function nor a distraction from the terminal function. Rather, GE exists to support the development of all students and not just those who are deemed fit for a liberal arts education or a bachelor's degree. GE evolves as student and community aspirations evolve. Over and over, Pusser and Levin construct the challenge of re-imagining the community college in terms of inquiry: colleges and students need to understand how curricular structures support students' actual learning aspirations, what kind of learning is happening, and what future pathways that learning does (and does not) open. Rather than the reproduction of an existing hierarchy of opportunity or talent, twenty-first-century GE is a process of inquiring into opportunity and developing talent in order to support students' general development.

Searching for Productive Inquiry: Promising Developments, Missed Opportunities

Are Midwestern two-year colleges and their partners beginning to construct GE curricula as inquiry into the needs of students and the region? How are these schools managing information concerning general learning and how are they facilitating reflection on growth inside and outside the college? Washbon's chapter in this volume suggests an obvious place to look. Washbon calls attention to successful programs in several Wisconsin technical colleges that have partnered with regional businesses and senior colleges to mediate the development of learners and the region. The focus here will be on the Radiology Technician Program at Great Lakes Technical College (GLTC, a pseudonym), one of the programs taught in the Health Education Center, an innovative site of collaboration between junior and senior colleges and a local community.

Two qualifications seem worth making here. First, in an attempt to read the program as it is articulated for potential learners rather than as the intentions of an institution, this analysis is limited to observations of the program as it appears in published documents. Clearly, a follow-up study might use other methods to explore the experiences of students in the program as well as the actual operationalization of the published program.

NEW DIRECTIONS FOR COMMUNITY COLLEGES • DOI: 10.1002/cc

Second, based on a variety of outcomes measures, this is a successful program. The missed opportunities described ahead are best understood as formal gaps in a still-evolving program.

This program is no longer a terminal associate degree and certification program. Radiology technicians are expected to develop a discrete set of skills and knowledge. That has not changed. However, in health-care settings, these technicians will also interact frequently as individuals and team members with specialists in engineering, public health, information technology, and other fields depending on the needs of their communities and clinics. They will learn and relearn the radiologic diagnostic tools and processes, as well as the use of databases and communication technologies. They will make note of the level of accuracy in following protocols with a wide range of patients. They will make judgments about ethical and cost-effective follow-up plans for further screening. They will be challenged to consider what knowledge or expertise they are missing and become aware of new information sources and continuing education or training opportunities, as demanded by their experiences with patients and physicians. They will also need to consider carefully the options and opportunities for further education in radiology or other fields.

In the rapidly changing economic and social context, the expectation of twenty-first-century community college learners is substantial. If a two-year program is to provide practice and assessment in all of these areas, every credit and learning experience will count. As Washbon's chapter suggests, the Wisconsin Technical College System (WTCS) institutions have thought carefully about what programs, certificates, and skills count for its region. The institutional mission links the college with its region, and the college places most of its graduates in the region. The Radiology Technician program realizes that mission through a "research-based curriculum which includes relevant concepts and theories reflecting current and future trends in clinical practice." Moreover, the program aims to produce graduates who will be "future leaders, clinicians, educators, and researchers with a goal." The program description underlines the fact that the program is "intellectually demanding" and that students need recent science course work to gain admission. The program Web page cites impressive data from the 2008–2009 Graduate Follow-up Study. Thirty-six graduates were earning on average $28 per hour in local clinics.

The program itself has an explicit and rigid curricular structure. Four semesters of classes are mapped out for students along with key examination and advising dates. While the core program experiences involve service learning and simulations, the "general education" experience is a set of courses that fall into traditional distribution areas. The traditional array of courses (selections from basic science, social science, communications, and multicultural studies) is taught by departments across the college. While the Radiology Technician program has stated GE outcomes in the program description, the general education requirements are not integrated with the core program courses. Students are encouraged to complete the GE courses before beginning the core program courses. Moreover, the core college outcomes and related learning indicators are not mentioned in connection with the GE requirement. These outcomes enter the experience of students in the program only when they are included in the classes taken before the program sequence begins in earnest.

Like other two-year colleges, GLTC has invested significant energy, driven in part by accreditation, in understanding student learning and success. The Community College Survey of Student Engagement (CCSSE) and the Student Satisfaction Inventory provide information about students' academic and social integration. The Inventory of Student Success database serves as a repository of information about student progress. Each of these inquiry efforts is indexed within the college's AQIP portfolio (an online database provided by the North Central Association of Colleges and Schools). Through self-report surveys, focus groups, program scorecards, and demographic data analyses, the college gathers information it can use to improve programs. Student learning is represented within this work as a set of core abilities, which align with the consensus standards. A commercial curriculum design system (Worldwide Instructional Design System) is used to align courses and assignments with the outcomes and indicators. These outcomes are infused across the curriculum (no outcome is the full responsibility of any one course) and integrated into the curriculum through syllabi. A high-level discussion of the core abilities on the college Web page offers this rationale:

> A high-level discussion of the core abilities on the college web page makes clear that GLTC aims to demonstrate and document student progress in a set of core abilities together with the mastery of a set of technical skills so as to establish that degrees add value to graduates' education and are aligned with employer expectations.

The review of the AQIP portfolio notes that "direct measures" of student learning are collected in a central database, though such measures are not listed in course and program descriptions and appear to be reported primarily as aggregate program success evidence. The program's Web site description of the core abilities encourages students to talk to their instructors or to call a central number for more information.

GLTC is building a culture of evidence in an institutional portfolio. The central site of public inquiry, the AQIP systems portfolio, provides little evidence of ongoing reflection by learners and teachers about general learning. While such reflection may well be going on, it does not appear to be guiding changes in the GE program. The assessment of general learning is centered on a set of indicators (COMPASS scores, grades, outcomes measures) that provide little space for teachers and learners to stop and consider both student performance and patterns in the GE data worthy of understanding for purposes of program improvement. Course descriptions within the Radiology Technician program pick up the language of the general learning indicators (critical thinking, problem solving, and so on) without reference to appropriate GE courses or an overview of the capacities required of "future leaders, clinicians, educators, and researchers with a program-related goal." While communication is a central value for the College's review process (and is one of the categories in the AQIP database), there appears to be little room for learners and teachers (and especially GE learners and teachers) to link their work to the broader GLTC aims.

Clearly the Radiology Technician program links technical education with the needs of a community. There is evidence that the program places students in well-paying jobs. Based on the published representation of general learning within the college, though, it is harder to determine whether these learners are being prepared to consider a broad spectrum of potential subsequent opportunities in radiation therapy, health-care leadership or management, or related pathways such as marketing or quality assurance. While a commitment to general learning is prominent in the two-year college's aims, that commitment is harder to find in the documents that describe this one program. The formal structure of its GE curriculum and the apparent lack of formal opportunities for learner and teacher reflection seem to limit attainment of the broader goals of transferable learning. While they may well exist, paths by which encounters between learners and teachers can lead to alternative ways of learning are not made visible in the program descriptions. In short, the innovation that led to the founding of the Health Science Center and the view that a radiation technician must be prepared to be not only a clinician but also an inquirer and innovator has not yet fully formally restructured the GLTC GE program.

Progress and Prospects for Advancing General Education

Deconstructing "traditional typologies of community college student aspirations" and constructing GE as inquiry into learning includes risks for program leaders and evaluators. In light of wide-ranging public policy interest in substantially improving postsecondary education completion rates and providing social mobility to an increasingly diverse clientele, the transferability and marketability of degrees and certificates remain crucial considerations for students and the regions in which they reside. Several of the chapters in this volume argue for alternative views of student development and institutional success; all agree that community and technical colleges need to enable students to gain the technical abilities and credentials needed at work and in college. Too much investment in inquiry into learning is potentially a distraction from the current policy agenda.

There is a growing sense in these chapters and in recent reviews of postsecondary education (Staley and Trinkle, 2011) that GE does need to change, to accelerate students' completion of programs and to bring education closer to the lives of students. But are we prepared to empower two-year college students to negotiate with the instructor of, hypothetically, a course on medical ethics about the usefulness of specific case analysis projects to enhance the student's capacity to function with a full set of ethical standards and insights in local health-care settings? Two-year colleges are getting closer to imagining some courses as project-based mash-ups in which faculty explicate college learning standards, suggest strategies and resources, provide feedback, and assess students' development. Yet, there remains some distance between these innovations and two-year college programs that empower and enable faculty to (1) reflect (with and apart from students) on what other kinds of learning and experiences need to take place for learners and the college to meet their goals, (2) decide whether more traditional courses are necessary, or (3) consider whether students are better served by other experiences in other programs. In far too many colleges, GE is defined in terms of transferable courses rather than as inquiry processes through which students and teachers produce new learning that benefits a local community and, by extension, students, colleges, and employers.

In short, GE is not widely viewed as an integral part of an apprenticeship aimed at developing wise learners who are prepared to contribute to their various communities—professional, civic, and personal. Within higher education as it is structured, an apprenticeship like the one suggested in the GE literature would not transfer well and would require levels of student–student, faculty–student, and faculty–faculty interaction that violate current expectations and norms, not to mention contracts. Other, less ambitious approaches that are more aligned with current policy will likely prevail, but any change that aims at meeting the demands of the twenty-first century will support inquiry into curricular structures that are relevant to student and institutional and public goals, ongoing assessment of student learning and success, and established reflection practices that seek to understand local development in regional and global terms. I will close with five provisional suggestions about how institutions might open GE to inquiry:

1. *Review GE as a curricular unit with a local mission and outcomes.* GE programs need to support the development of the students who have been admitted to an institution rather than provide students who are already qualified to transfer with credits that will transfer into one or another discipline. While GE outcomes must be carefully integrated with broader institutional and departmental outcomes, GE programs are necessarily focused on providing access and support in a local context.
2. *Publish student work and reflections.* Grades from traditional GE courses say little about the kinds of inquiry experiences students have had or the use they made of those experiences; student work and reflections

reveal to both internal and external stakeholders how students have developed as inquirers and what developmental experiences are productive next steps.

3. *Study the attitudes and inquiry practices of GE faculty and students.* Making GE programs part of a twenty-first-century education entails understanding and challenging myths—GE is something to get out of the way—and enables GE faculty to document student success.

4. *Track student movement through GE and into specialized inquiry experiences.* If GE programs are to provide students with opportunities to practice inquiry that transfers across academic and occupational settings, the managers of GE programs have to follow students to those settings to ensure that GE opportunities lead to transferable education.

5. *Establish local, regional, and national educational pathways for students.* The literature reviewed earlier predicts that locally relevant GE will be increasingly interdisciplinary and collaborative and often acquired outside classrooms in research or service learning settings. Program administrators need to build networks that value students' capacity to do inquiry and not only the educational experiences captured on their transcripts.

Notes

1. I will use *two-year college* and *community college* to refer to comprehensive community colleges, institutions that offer career and technical programs as well as transfer programs. I make the generalization with some concern, well aware that individual institutions have developed varied missions that, in a larger study, should be differentiated. Unfortunately, studies of community colleges often fail to acknowledge the complexities and competing interests created by diverse college missions (Bailey and Morest, 2004).

2. This article initially included a fully documented review of this discussion. A more extensive bibliography is available from the author.

3. As a result, the topic resists boundaries. GE has in Western tradition alone three millennia of continuous history. The study of GE considers not only institutions and curricula and learning but ethical questions about what an educated citizen is. I will use the acronym GE to separate this historical concept from more commonsensical descriptors, such as "general education," "core courses," or even "liberal education."

References

Association of American Colleges and Universities (AAC&U). "College Learning for the New Global Century." 2007. Retrieved November 10, 2009, from http://www.aacu .org/advocacy/leap/documents/GlobalCentury_final.pdf

Bailey, T., and Morest, V. S. "The Organizational Efficiency of Multiple Missions for Community Colleges." Research Report. New York: Community College Research Center, Teachers College, Columbia University, February 2004.

Barr, R. B., and Tagg, J. "From Teaching to Learning: A New Paradigm for Undergraduate Education." *Change*, 1995, 27, 12–25.

Bragg, D. "The New Vocationalism in Community Colleges." *New Directions for Community Colleges*, 2001, 115, 5–15.

Bransford, J. D., Brown, A. L., and Cocking, R. R. (eds.). *How People Learn: Brain, Mind, Experience, and School.* Expanded edition. Washington, D.C.: National Academy Press, 2000.

Brint, S. G., and Karabel, J. *The Diverted Dream: Community Colleges and the Promise of Educational Opportunity in America, 1900–1985.* New York: Oxford University Press, 1989.

Cohen, A. M., and Ignash, J. M. "An Overview of the Total Credit Curriculum." *New Directions for Community Colleges,* 1994, *86,* 13–29.

Conrad, C., and Wyer, J. C. *Liberal Education in Transition.* Washington, D.C.: ERIC Clearinghouse on Higher Education & American Association for Higher Education, 1980.

Gee, J. P. *Situated Language and Learning: A Critique of Traditional Schooling.* New York: Routledge, 2004.

Gibbons, M., Limoges, C., Nowotny, H., Schwartzman, S., Scott, P., and Trow, M. *The New Production of Knowledge: The Dynamics of Science and Research in Contemporary Societies.* Thousand Oaks, Calif.: SAGE Publications, 1999.

Johnson, D. K., Ratcliff, J. L., and Gaff, J. G. "A Decade of Change in General Education." *New Directions for Higher Education,* 2004, *125,* 9–28.

Kress, G. R. *Literacy in the New Media Age.* London: Routledge, 2003.

McClenney, K. M. "Keeping America's Promises: Challenges for Community Colleges." In K. Boswell and C. D. Wilson (eds.), *Keeping America's Promise: A Report on the Future of the Community College.* Denver: Education Commission of the States and League for Innovation in the Community College, 2004.

Miles, C. L., and Wilson, C. "Learning Outcomes for the Twenty-First Century: Cultivating Student Success for College and the Knowledge Economy." *New Directions for Community Colleges,* 2004, *126,* 87–100.

Pusser, B., and Levin, J. "Re-Imagining Community Colleges in the 21st Century: A Student-Centered Approach to Higher Education." 2009. Retrieved February 15, 2011, from http://www.americanprogress.org/issues/2009/12/pdf/community_colleges_reimagined.pdf

Staley, D. J., and Trinkle, D. A. "The Changing Landscape of Higher Education." *Educause Review,* January–February 2011, 16–32.

University of California Commission on General Education. "General Education in the 21st Century." Berkeley: Center for Studies in Higher Education, 2007.

TODD C. LUNDBERG *is a Ph.D. student and graduate research associate in Educational Leadership and Policy Analysis at the University of Wisconsin–Madison; he was a founding faculty member at Cascadia Community College.*

8

This chapter examines the nation's changing research and innovation context and presents an evolving template for community college–research university partnerships, one grounded in Midwestern undergraduate student research experiences, faculty development initiatives, and new transfer partnerships.

Community College–Research University Collaboration: Emerging Student Research and Transfer Partnerships

L. Allen Phelps, Amy Prevost

In settings across the United States, governing boards, state officials, and campus leaders are intensely examining, refining, and reprioritizing postsecondary education missions and spending to optimize value-added economic and social returns. Recently, the National Governors Association (2008) suggested that states develop new postsecondary education compacts to include

> an innovation compact with major R&D universities. The compact would define long-term goals to address state needs, establish a system of accountability, and tie funding and autonomy to performance in meeting compact goals. Special attention should be paid to research universities and their role in commercialization and entrepreneurship.

In this chapter, we discuss the nation's changing research and innovation context, the emerging rationale for community college–research university partnerships, and selected innovative practices for engaging undergraduates and faculty members in research collaborations and transfer initiatives. We conclude with an analysis of the challenges confronting the broad-scale implementation of two-year college–research university partnerships.

NEW DIRECTIONS FOR COMMUNITY COLLEGES, no. 157, Spring 2012 © 2012 Wiley Periodicals, Inc.
Published online in Wiley Online Library (wileyonlinelibrary.com) • DOI: 10.1002/cc.20009

The Changing Research and Innovation Context

Clearly, strengthening the nation's research capacity is central to national and global economic growth. Recent econometric evidence, as well as federal investment strategies and state economic growth benchmarks, continue to emphasize the importance of building both research and innovation capacities in states and communities to sustain a globally competitive economy. Only recently have policymakers and postsecondary education leaders acknowledged and begun developing strategies for two-year college–research university collaborations.

The leading U.S. research universities have a remarkable economic impact. According to the American Association of Universities (n.d.), each year research institutions educate more than one million undergraduates, 430,000 graduate students, and 77,000 professional students; spend $121 billion; and license or patent thousands of discoveries that lead to new innovations, products, and companies.

As noted in the White House's Recovery Act Fourth Quarter Report:

> To ensure that America remains a world leader in innovation and technological discovery, President Obama announced in April 2009 the goal of boosting total national research and development (R&D) expenditures to 3 percent of GDP. As a down payment on that effort, the Recovery Act is providing $18 billion for scientific research—$10 billion for cutting-edge medical research through the National Institutes of Health, $3 billion to the National Science Foundation, and funding for research programs at NASA, the Department of Commerce, and the Department of Defense.[1]

Beyond the federal investment in scientific discovery and an increased research and development commitment from the president, the states are equally concerned with tracking economic changes and transformation. Created in 1999 by the Kaufmann Foundation and the Information Technology and Innovation Foundation, the 2010 State New Economy Index (SNEI) uses twenty-six indicators in five categories to benchmark the economic transformation of states. Since its creation, the SNEI has provided a score for each state on each of the twenty-six indicators. The five categories, the indicators, and the weighting factors used to generate the composite scores for each state are presented in Table 8.1.

The critical importance of expanding innovation or research capacity (e.g., venture capital, patents, or industry R&D investment) and increasing the proportion of knowledge-intensive jobs (e.g., IT professionals, workforce education level, share of the workforce in professional, managerial, and technical jobs) is strongly affirmed by these two categories and fourteen indicators driving nearly 55 percent of each state's composite index score. A cursory analysis of the 2010 report reveals that in the midst of a national recession, sixteen states increased their state rank from the 2007

Table 8.1.   2010 State New Economy Index, Performance Indicators
and Weights

Performance Indicators	Weight
KNOWLEDGE JOBS	
IT Professionals	0.75
Professional and Managerial Jobs	0.75
Workforce Education	1.00
Immigration of Knowledge Workers	0.50
U.S. Migration of Knowledge Workers	0.50
Manufacturing Value-Added	0.75
Traded-Services Employment	0.75
Total	5.00
GLOBALIZATION	
Export Focus on Manufacturing and Services	1.00
FDI	1.00
Total	2.00
ECONOMIC DYNAMISM	
Job Churning	1.00
IPOs	0.50
Entrepreneurial Activity	0.75
Inventor Patents	0.50
Fastest-Growing Firms	0.75
Total	3.50
DIGITAL ECONOMY	
Online Population	0.50
Digital Government	0.50
Farms and Technology	0.50
Broadband	1.00
Health IT	0.50
Total	3.00
INNOVATION Capacity	
High-Tech Employment	0.75
Scientists and Engineers	0.75
Patents	0.75
Industry R&D	1.00
Non-industry R&D	0.50
Green Economy	0.50
Venture Capital	0.75
Total	5.00

ranking in Knowledge Jobs (four states), Innovation Capacity (six states), or both (six states). Three of the sixteen states (Illinois, Ohio, and Missouri) are in the eight-state Midwest region, which provides some noteworthy benchmarking capacity for other Midwestern states to compare state-level strategies or policies used to increase knowledge jobs and innovation capacity.

As suggested by the SNEI indicators, community colleges have a prominent role in raising the state's workforce development capacity. The capacity for creating knowledge-based jobs is directly affected by the degree and certificate completion rates, as well as by successful transfer programs for students pursuing professional, managerial, or technical careers, including programs preparing IT professionals and technicians. Effective workplace training programs funded by employers and government help firms put new technologies into production environments while also raising the overall education level of the state's workforce. Through the rapidly expanding *science, technology, engineering,* and *mathematics* (STEM) programs, two-year colleges are an increasingly vital partner in raising the percentage of engineers and scientists in the workforce.

The New State Economy Index provides preliminary evidence and a set of metrics with face validity for advancing the alignment of postsecondary education systems with regional economic growth objectives and priorities within states and regions.

Framing the Options: New Roles for Community College–Research University Partnerships

The challenges in building effective collaborative arrangements and creating the necessary incentives in the postsecondary education community were cogently described by Gordon Gee, president of Ohio State University, in a recent interview in *Time*:

> The many elements of American higher ed—from community colleges to the giant research universities—operate as rival duchies and neglected colonies rather than as players on a single team. People look at me like I am crazy when I say that our greatest partnership here at Ohio State should be with the community colleges. We're all part of the same mission, which is education from pre-K through life. [Von Drehle, November 21, 2009, p. 48]

Making a similar argument in 2006 for greater postsecondary education coherence and alignment nationally, Education Secretary Margaret Spellings' Commission examining the future of American higher education recommended changes in policies and practices that would create a world-class twenty-first-century higher education system that

- Creates new knowledge, contributes to economic prosperity and global competitiveness, and empowers citizens
- Is accessible to all Americans throughout their lives
- Provides high-quality instruction to students while improving their efficiency in order to be more affordable to the students, taxpayers, and donors who sustain them

- Gives Americans the workplace skills they need to adapt to a rapidly changing economy
- Adapts to a world altered by technology, changing demographics, and globalization

More recently, the Brookings Metropolitan Policy Program (Simon, Foster, and Austin, 2010) cited a number of key assets and strategic advantages available in the Great Lakes region. Specifically, the twenty-one largest Great Lakes metropolitan communities are home to thirty-two major research universities. According to the National Science Foundation (NSF), these universities (1) educate 36 and 37 percent, respectively, of the nation's science and engineering undergraduate and graduate students; (2) educate 84,000 foreign students annually, who spend $2.3 billion in tuition and living expenses; and (3) were responsible for 33 percent of the nation's university and industry research expenditures in 2006.

The authors contend:

> Great Lakes universities are well-positioned to become major players in the global marketplace, addressing such challenges as global energy, food, water security, health care and medicine, and human capital development.

In the midst of rapidly declining state support for research, low in-state tuition, financial aid, and infrastructure costs, state and postsecondary education leaders lack incentives to view their assets as producing a regional or national economic development contribution. Rapidly, these circumstances create conditions that are inadequate to meet state goals and concurrently fail to address national or global competitive priorities. To address these complex challenges, the Brookings authors call for a new federal initiative modeled on the Land-Grant vision of 1862, known as the World-Grant mission. Their vision would establish a competitive grant program supported jointly by the federal government and foundations for consortia of universities and their partners to describe:

- The size and global scope of their research mission and achievements
- Their success in graduating students in disciplines critical to international competitiveness
- Their demonstrated commitment to international engagement, outreach, and the co-creation of knowledge, research partnerships, and learning exchanges
- A commitment to local (metro community) and broader regional (e.g., Great Lakes industrial communities) engagement and impact through technology and innovation development, entrepreneurial efforts, and partnerships with other knowledge centers (e.g., K-through-12 schools, community colleges, regional universities, research organizations)

Table 8.2.   Relationships between Selected High-Impact Activities and
Clusters of Effective Educational Practices

	Level of Academic Challenge	Active and Collaborative Learning	Student-Faculty Interaction	Supportive Campus Environment
First-Year				
Learning Communities	++	+++	+++	++
Service Learning	++	+++	+++	++
Senior				
Study Abroad	++	++	++	+
Student-Faculty Research	+++	+++	+++	++
Service Learning	++	+++	+++	++
Senior Culminating Experience	++	++	+++	++

+ p < .001, ++ p < .001 & Unstd B > .10, +++ p < .001 & Unstd B > .30
Source: High-Impact Educational Practices: What They Are, Who Has Access to Them, and Why They Matter by George D. Kuh (Washington, DC: AAC&U, 2008). For information and more resources and research from LEAP, see www.aacu.org/leap.

Most importantly, the new roles for community college–research university partnerships can be anchored in student learning. Kuh's analysis of high-impact educational practices in colleges and universities identifies "undergraduate research" experiences as a key factor influencing student engagement and retention (2008). Using National Surveys of Student Engagement (NSSE) data from college seniors, undergraduate research experiences were reported consistently across institutions receiving the highest scores on the four NSSE engagement benchmark scales (see Table 8.2).

Kuh describes the importance of undergraduate research as a vital ingredient for college student learning in the twenty-first century:

Undergraduate Research

Many colleges and universities are now providing research experiences for students in all disciplines. Undergraduate research, however, has been most prominently used in science disciplines. With strong support from the National Science Foundation and the research community, scientists are reshaping their courses to connect key concepts and questions with students' early and active involvement in systematic investigation and research. The goal is to involve students with actively contested questions, empirical observation, cutting-edge technologies, and the sense of excitement that comes from working to answer important questions.

In the following section, we summarize various community college undergraduate research initiatives and projects designed to enhance transfer, as well as other research and teaching collaborations among two-year and four-year institutions.

Leveraging Promising Innovations: Selected Undergraduate Research and Transfer Initiatives

This section describes several Midwestern innovative collaborations involving students, faculty members, and new institutional arrangements.[2]

Undergraduate Research Programs: STEM Engines. This NSF-supported Undergraduate Research Collaborative in Chemistry is anchored in a partnership between ten Chicago-area two-year colleges (2YCs) and three regional baccalaureate-granting institutions. The Collaborative, now in its fourth year of a five-year grant, is to explore new models of authentic undergraduate research that engage 2YC students, make them aware of career opportunities in the STEM disciplines, and ultimately propel them into scientific careers.

Rigorous undergraduate research experiences for students on both the two-year campus and four-year campus during the summer are featured. Additionally, the selected students are part of a regional scholarly community, which strengthens their learning and growth as scientists, enables them to develop a professional mentoring network, builds their leadership and time management competencies, and supports new research collaborations. As shown in Figure 8.1, four models for undergraduate research are being developed across the partnership institutions.

The STEM-Engines Collaborative encourages students and faculty members to present their findings at national conferences and in peer-reviewed journals. So far, six students have coauthored articles published in the chemistry and biotechnology journals. Additionally, ninety-five students have presented their work at professional meetings such as the American Chemical Society.

Several Midwestern institutions are involved in the NSF's "science-focused" Community College Research Initiative, including the University of Wisconsin–Barron County and several community colleges in Minnesota: North Hennepin Community College, Akon-Ramsey Community College, and Riverland Community College. These community colleges work in conjunction with the University of Wisconsin–LaCrosse and the University of Minnesota, along with other four-year partners.

Students engage in research projects by joining ongoing research teams to ask questions that have readily understood applications. For example, a project from the Rochester Institute of Technology is focused on studying the population genetics of raptors in North America. Students collect whole blood from captured specimens and sequence the DNA of these animals to gain a better understanding of the subspecies validity (between species cap-

Figure 8.1. Models for Undergraduate Research in Chemistry

Scaffolded training. This model adapts the traditional student–faculty mentor relationship to the needs of 2YC students and builds their confidence and abilities through a scaffolded undergraduate research experience. Students and faculty mentors develop a research question that is mutually interesting and appropriate for the student's abilities.

Interdisciplinary team research. Students are enrolled in a formal research course and receive academic credit. Working with an interdisciplinary team of 2YC faculty, students formulate their own research questions, conduct their own literature reviews, and work in teams to design, implement, and evaluate their own experiments from an interdisciplinary perspective.

Distributed team research. A hybrid of the other two, this model aims to have small teams of students at separate campuses working in parallel on a mutually interesting research question.

Summer research experiences for undergraduates. Students participate in the research culture at the campus of their choice during a ten-week internship.

tured in the Rochester, New York, area and those captured in the Duluth, Minnesota, area) and to create a relationship tree for these raptors. This allows students to use their knowledge of molecular biology, particularly of DNA structure and functions, and the techniques used to study DNA (Polymerase chain reaction (PCR) and DNA sequencing), as well as concepts such as population genetics).

Research Experiences for Community College Faculty: A Boston–Metro Collaborative.   Despite the challenges of negotiating the research university's size and complexity, meaningful partnerships between community colleges and research universities have developed through Research Experiences for Teachers (RET) programs. These NSF grants provide community college faculty members with six- to eight-week summer research experiences on university campuses working with university faculty in research projects. In addition to research, the faculty member also becomes part of a network that provides continuing access to professional development opportunities and a forum for sharing relevant information and publications. These programs provide innovative ways to enhance both teaching and learning at the community college and at the university.

Northeastern University, in collaboration with Boston University and the University of Massachusetts–Lowell, has operated a Research Experience for Teachers program since 2006 with a grant from the NSF Engineering Research Centers (ERC). In this program a minimum of ten participants per year from both local K-through-12 school districts and community colleges from anywhere in the United States come together with faculty from Northeastern University, Boston University (both private research universities), and the University of Massachusetts–Lowell (a public four-year university, part of the UMass system with a national reputation in science, engineering, and technology) for six weeks of research on one of the university campuses. Participants work a minimum of thirty-five hours per week conducting research, completing additional activities related to their research such as project team meetings, seminars, and special training sessions, keeping a detailed laboratory research notebook, and creating a research poster presentation to present to colleagues at the end of the session. Further, participants complete activities outside of their laboratory work related to meeting the goals of the RET program, such as keeping a journal for reflection, attending RET meetings, and going on field trips. Participants are paid as temporary employees of Northeastern University. An outline of the lesson plan and curriculum connection will be shared at the final meeting of the summer. To date, sixty-five students (referred to as *teachers* by the Northeastern RET program) have been involved. Of these, roughly 10 percent are community college faculty. Although these faculty can come from anywhere in the United States, they generally come from nearby institutions.

The goals of the RET at Northeastern are to encourage participants and mentor faculty to (1) engage in collaborative inquiry through shared research experiences, (2) strengthen the content knowledge of teachers, (3) build understanding and professional aspect, and (4) provide opportunities for leadership and professional development for all members of the RET team. A recent article in the journal *Science* (Silverstein and others, 2009) reviews the benefits for students of teachers who have engaged in research programs. Some findings include teachers' better appreciation for students' struggles with content, increased hands-on content of the curriculum, and the inclusion of new laboratory experiences in the curriculum as well as the introduction of new technology. Also, teachers are more likely to lead students in discussions of science careers and to include scientific journal articles in their curriculum. In addition to these benefits, the program offers an opportunity for participants to review and select research-based curriculum programs or units that are aligned with local, state, and national frameworks. The use of a blog keeps participants up to date on professional development opportunities and allows them to share current information with each other. There are additional opportunities to meet with each other at national conferences such as the National Science Teachers' Association (NSTA) meeting.

In the 2010 RET granting cycle, more institutions have engaged community college faculty as participants in their RET programs. Norman Fortenberry, a principal investigator on an RET project at the National Academy of Sciences, describes the importance of community colleges as an essential component of the nation's science and technology pipeline:

NEW DIRECTIONS FOR COMMUNITY COLLEGES • DOI: 10.1002/cc

Within the engineering and engineering technology communities, the most critical role of community colleges is as feeders to baccalaureate engineering and engineering technology programs. Indeed, some states (e.g., California and Florida) explicitly depend on community colleges as a key pathway for students seeking baccalaureate degrees in all fields. [National Academy of Sciences, 2010]

In addition to research, participants in RETs from community colleges also engage in activities such as comparison of statewide curricula and assessment rubrics. At the University of Maryland, one project involves the comparison and alignment of statewide community college courses (e.g., Introduction to Engineering) to similarly titled introductory courses offered by the University of Maryland–College Park. As part of the summer research program, community college faculty members compare their courses with syllabi, design projects, and laboratories with those in the Materials Science and Engineering Program at the University of Maryland. In addition, the faculty members gather exemplary design projects created by 2YC engineering students and apply a newly developed portfolio-based scoring rubric that provides a concurrent benchmark for comparing courses and student learning.

At Stanford, Dr. Sheri Sheppard has developed a Research Experience for Teachers in the Bay Area. As part of the experience, attendees develop curricula to use at their institutions, in addition to working in labs and attending lectures on both scientific and education topics. One unique feature of this program is that in addition to a stipend offered to teachers for attending ($7,200), an additional amount of money ($1,000) is granted to each attendee after he or she implements the newly developed curricula with students. Stated goals of the program are to re-inspire teachers by allowing them to experience hands-on research and revisit academia. This helps teachers and community college instructors learn about new areas of scientific research and supports them in their role in preparing the next generation of scientists and engineers.

Strengthening Transfer Success: Research University Initiatives

The myriad challenges of transfer pathways that face 2YC transfer students were addressed by Melguizo and Dowd (2006). In reviewing national longitudinal data from the high school class of 1992, they found that, contrary to conventional thinking, the more competitive the four-year institution, the more likely a transfer student is to graduate from that institution. Those community college transfers who enrolled at highly selective and selective four-year institutions graduated in high numbers. Seventy-five percent completed their degrees within 8.5 years, a figure that increases to 80 or 90 percent at elite institutions. The authors contend that highly competitive institutions provide more opportunities for individualized interaction with faculty and more personalized advising services. This outcome suggests that connected undergraduate student research opportunities and cross-institutional faculty collaborations may be enhancing the post-transfer success of students. These connections are explored in the development of new transfer programs, such as the UW–Madison and Madison College's Engineering Blueprint program.

Launched in 2009, the University of Wisconsin–Madison College of Engineering (UW–COE) and Madison (Area Technical) College's (MATC) Blueprint program provides transferring students with a number of strategic advantages. More than just a transfer program, Blueprint is a collaboration between UW–COE and MATC faculty, which has resulted in the joint faculty development of new courses that transfer to UW–COE. New MATC introductory courses have been developed in engineering design, computer engineering, engineering statistics, engineering graphics, and differential equations.

If MATC students meet the Blueprint requirements, they are guaranteed admission to their specified engineering degree program of interest (from among ten listed programs), excepting some limited-capacity programs (e.g., biomedical engineering, chemical engineering, and engineering physics). Students interested in those programs can apply for admission as regular transfer students. MATC students interested in the limited-capacity majors apply to MATC as liberal arts transfer students.

To participate in the Blueprint program, students must be enrolled as first-year college students at MATC and sign a Declaration of Intent to Participate form prior to the completion of twenty-four college transfer credits at MATC. They must specify the engineering degree program at UW–Madison they wish to enter, at which time they become Engineering Transfer Blueprint candidates.

Once admitted, first- and second-semester transfer students qualify for free one-to-one tutoring. MATC students must fulfill the minimum requirements for admission to UW–Madison. That is, they must complete the College of Engineering admission requirements with at least a 2.5 grade point average (GPA) in specified math and science courses, and an overall MATC GPA of at least a 3.0 in all college transfer courses. Students who successfully complete these requirements are guaranteed admission to one of UW–Madison's participating engineering degree-granting programs. The UW–MATC faculty collaboration has integrated the Blueprint course requirements into the suggested two-year curriculum at MATC. The first year includes a recommended course, Introduction to Engineering Design, which helps students explore the profession and obtain hands-on experience with a client-centered engineering design project. The curriculum sheet also includes additional recommended courses that may be used to fulfill COE degree requirements depending on the student's specified engineering program.

Since January 2009, sixty-four MATC students have been admitted to the Blueprint program. In addition, the demand for first-year calculus and analytical geometry courses has increased substantially, suggesting that undeclared and unadmitted students are exploring the program and pathway informally.

The Leverage Challenges

Fulfilling the National Governors Association's vision (2008) for state postsecondary education compacts that capitalize on the intellectual resources of major R&D universities is a multidimensional challenge. As this and other chapters in the volume suggest, new federal and state policies are needed to enhance the capacity for two-year college–research university collaboration in technology transfer, entrepreneurial innovation, and developing a future workforce with the skills and knowledge to support discovery, research, and continuous innovation.

Some important capacity-building lessons have been reported in recent studies. After examining a limited but growing number of undergraduate research programs at community colleges for three years, the Council on Undergraduate Research (Hensel, 2010) offered several recommendations for developing a culture of research and inquiry to affect students' learning and enhance institutional partnerships:

- Boards of trustees need to recognize that engaging students in research is a legitimate and powerful teaching strategy. Boards need to affirm the interests of faculty members in engaging in research and support the efforts of students to do so.
- Community colleges should expand their partnerships with nearby four-year colleges, local industries, and local government and nonprofit agencies to provide additional research opportunities for students.
- Community college administrators need to support and encourage faculty members' involvement in their disciplinary or professional organizations so that professors can remain current in their fields and be aware of future directions.
- Community college administrators also need to find ways of supporting faculty members for outside-the-classroom mentoring of students engaged in collaborative research.
- Faculty members need to consider ways in which the development of research skills can be incorporated into the curriculum.
- Student-affairs personnel at community colleges need to recognize the importance of undergraduate research for students' transfer and career opportunities and encourage students to participate in research activities.
- Local employers need to provide research opportunities for community college students as well as students from four-year institutions.

- Community college administrators need to provide support for faculty members to write proposals for external funding.

Similar recommendations were generated by Bailey and Alfonso (2005) while investigating the research on the program's effectiveness in the nation's community colleges. They argued that the research and evaluation capacity at two-year colleges will have an influence only when it is used in day-to-day decision-making on campuses. They suggest that (1) community college faculty and administrators must have wider opportunities to engage in the research, (2) research findings must be widely disseminated to inform practice and policy, and (3) interinstitutional research collaboration with other colleges and between state-level researchers must be promoted.

Implications for Practice

Two-year college leaders and instructors interested in developing or advancing student research opportunities and transfer partnerships with research universities should be cognizant of the regional assets for such initiatives. These assets include but are not limited to the following:

- National concerns about investment in scientific discovery and the expansion of research and innovation capacity are echoed at the regional and state level. The role of community and technical colleges is crucial for developing a regional knowledge-based workforce.
- Program alignment must be achieved between community colleges, high schools, and four-year and research universities, especially in high-wage, knowledge-worker sectors, such as STEM and Health Sciences, where research-based knowledge and skills are critical to success.
- Similarly, as illustrated in this chapter, creating or expanding community college programs and career pathways that allow students to become early and active participants in systematic investigation and research helps to optimize student engagement and development.

References

American Association of Universities. (n.d.) "Economic Impacts of AAU Universities." Retrieved March 27, 2011, from http://www.aau.edu/research/article.aspx?id=9266
Bailey, T., and Alfonso, M. "Paths to Persistence: An Analysis of research on Program Effectiveness at Community Colleges." New Agenda Series, 2005, 6(1). Indianapolis, Ind.: Lumina Foundation for Education. Retrieved March 27, 2011, from http://www.luminafoundation.org/publications/PathstoPersistence.pdf
Hensel, N. "Undergraduate Research at Community Colleges: Context, Implications, and Recommendations." Washington, D.C.: Council on Undergraduate Education, 2010. Retrieved March 27, 2011, from http://www.cur.org/urcc/ch7-03.html

Kuh, G. D. "High-Impact Educational Practices: What They Are, Who Has Access to Them, and Why They Matter." Washington, D.C.: Association of American Colleges and Universities, 2008. Retrieved March 27, 2011, from https://secure.aacu.org/source /Orders/index.cfm?section=unknown&task=3&CATEGORY=LEAP&PRODUCT_TYP E=SALES&SKU=HIGHIMP&DESCRIPTION=&FindSpec=&CFTOKEN=43290727& continue=1&SEARCH_TYPE=

Melguizo, T., and Dowd, A. C. "National Estimates of Transfer Access and Baccalaureate Degree Attainment at Four-Year Colleges and Universities." Los Angeles: Jack Cooke Kent Foundation, 2006. Retrieved April 1, 2011, from www.jkcf.org/assets /files/0000/0196/Section_I.pdf

National Academy of Sciences (2010). Award abstract, Federal Award ID 1042875, http://www.nasonline.org/, retrieved 09/15/2010.

National Governors Association. "Innovation America: A Compact for Postsecondary Education." Washington, D.C.: Author, 2008. Retrieved March 27, 2011, from http:// www.nga.org/Files/pdf/0707INNOVATIONPOSTSEC.PDF

Silverstein, S.C., Dubner, J., Miller, J. Glied, S. and Loike, J.D. (2009). Teachers' Participation in Research Programs Improves Their Students' Achievement in Science. *Science, 326*(5951), 440–442.

Simon, L. A., Foster, R. M., and Austin, J. "The Federal Role in Supporting Public Universities' Global Missions." Washington, D.C.: Metropolitan Policy Program, The Brookings Institution, 2010. Retrieved March 27, 2011, from http://www.brookings .edu/~/media/Files/rc/papers/2010/0927_great_lakes/0927_great_lakes_papers/0927 _great_lakes_higher_education.pdf

Von Drehle, D. "The Big Man on Campus." *Time*, November 21, 2009, *174*(20), 44–48.

Notes

1. Web references for the innovative programs described herein are available upon request: please contact Amy Prevost at aprevost@wisc.edu.
2. Program references available upon request: please contact Amy Prevost at aprevost@ wisc.edu.

L. ALLEN PHELPS *is professor emeritus of Educational Leadership and Policy Analysis and former director of the Center on Education and Work at the University of Wisconsin–Madison.*

AMY PREVOST *is the director of Scientific Courses at the BioPharmaceutical Technology Center Institute, located in Madison, Wisconsin.*

NEW DIRECTIONS FOR COMMUNITY COLLEGES • DOI: 10.1002/cc

9

In this chapter we propose a framework to guide innovators and change agents in two-year colleges. Leaders of these efforts are encouraged to choose strategies based in part on the impetus and focus of the change effort, including regional alliance opportunities.

A Framework and Strategies for Advancing Change and Innovation in Two-Year Colleges

Christopher J. Matheny, Clifton Conrad

Notwithstanding variation in institutional missions, two-year colleges are the gateway to postsecondary education for the majority of college and university students in this country. As institutions of choice for many and institutions of necessity for others, two-year institutions are constantly challenged to meet the rapidly changing needs of diverse constituencies and multiple stakeholders. While two-year colleges often pride themselves in being uniquely positioned to respond to the changing needs of their communities, bringing about major change and innovation remains a formidable challenge. Nested in this context, the purpose of this chapter is to address the following question: What strategies, under what conditions, are most promising with respect to successfully bringing about change and innovation in two-year colleges in the Midwest? Particular attention is given to change and innovation strategies implemented in emerging regional partnerships.

Traditionally, most academic reform and structural change have taken place largely through accretion and attrition. However, in the rapidly changing landscape of the twenty-first century as to market forces, changes in demographics, globalization, and postmodern ideals regarding investment in public infrastructure, external forces are driving much of the change and innovation in higher education. In turn, it is not surprising that the literature on models of change, innovation, and reform in two-year

NEW DIRECTIONS FOR COMMUNITY COLLEGES, no. 157, Spring 2012 © 2012 Wiley Periodicals, Inc.
Published online in Wiley Online Library (wileyonlinelibrary.com) • DOI: 10.1002/cc.20010

colleges increasingly refers to external forces as the primary drivers of change in two-year institutions. Still, whether the primary drivers of change are external or internal, leaders in two-year colleges need strategies for successfully bringing about change and innovation both within their institutions and across the regions of the country they serve.

We anchor this chapter in the proposition that no single model of change in the extant literature is sufficient by itself to help educational leaders in two-year colleges successfully bring about change and innovation. We suggest that a blending of models and accompanying strategies can best equip leaders at all levels, from the regional to the institutional, in successfully navigating change. More specifically, we suggest that the models and strategies that are the most likely to be effective hinge on two major considerations: first, whether the impetus for change comes from inside or outside of the organization, and second, whether the locus of the change is the institution or across the respective region, such as the Midwest. Responses to these two considerations can help leaders frame change in terms of the major change models identified in the literature and in turn choose strategies that are most likely to be effective.

This chapter is composed of four parts. We begin by reviewing the major models advanced in the literature on academic change. Next, we examine which of these models seem most promising for application in two-year colleges. We then advance a holistic framework, one that incorporates all of these models, as a heuristic for initiating and implementing major change in two-year colleges. Finally, drawing on the models nested within this overarching framework, we identify various change strategies associated with each of the four quadrants that comprise our model, followed by a brief description of a change effort that exemplifies the strategies associated with the respective quadrant. Throughout, our animating intent is not to endorse specific changes but rather to invite reflection on change strategies in ways that can help leaders to bring about meaningful change and innovation in two-year colleges.

Models of Change*

As elaborated on in Kezar's (2001) comprehensive review of academic change and innovation in higher education, six major models have been advanced in the literature on change and innovation in higher education: evolutionary, planned, political, life-cycle, social cognition, and cultural. Notwithstanding other classifications and typologies that have been advanced, Kezar's six models provide a useful typology of the models of

*The authors acknowledge the many scholars who have contributed to this rich body of research. For the convenience of the reader, parenthetical references are held to a minimum in this chapter. A full list of references of the studies supporting the models of change and implications for two-year college leadership strategies is available from the lead author.

change and innovation. Before elaborating on these six models, it is important to note that, viewed on a continuum, evolutionary (adaptive) change models and planned-change models occupy, as the terms suggest, the poles of *reactive change* versus *planned change* and are the most prevalent in the literature, with the other four models (political, life-cycle, social cognition, and cultural) each occupying some middle ground between planned change and reactive change.

Evolutionary or adaptive models focus on organizational responses to environmental stimuli, with organizations viewed within the context of their environment. From this perspective, changes in the environment lead to organizational discomfort, and in turn organizational change is the response intended to bring the organization back to homeostasis—a steady state between the organization and the environment. In broad strokes, evolutionary change models draw heavily on biological and scientific models of change in which incremental change and mutation over time determine the success or failure of the organism (organization). In effect, change is viewed as a natural progression as systems self-organize and evolve over time. At the same time, this slow evolution may be punctuated by periods of extreme discontinuity in which significant changes in the environment force organizations to quickly and radically adapt or face the prospect of extinction. Whereas most work on adaptive change focuses on change at the organizational level, there is some precedent for using adaptive change frameworks to explain the change process at a regional or industry level. Meyer, Brooks, and Goes (1990) use an adaptive change framework to examine the change process within individual hospitals and the industry as a whole. Their research suggests that strategies for bringing about change differ depending on the type of change (incremental versus revolutionary) and the focus of the change (firm versus industry-wide).

In sharp contrast to evolutionary or adaptive models, *planned-change models* stress rational, highly linear approaches to the initiation and implementation of change that is driven primarily by internal factors or agents. Planned-change models draw attention to an organization's ability to motivate change through intentional decision making, goal setting, and execution of specific change strategies, resulting in new organizational structures, products, practices, and policies. Because planned-change models have an internal locus of control, leadership is critical to the change process. In these models, external forces may ultimately factor into planned change, but environmental influences are typically not antecedent to bringing about change. Most students of change and innovation in higher education suggest that the application of planned-change models, such as through strategic planning, require some modification in professional bureaucracies such as colleges and universities in light of the participatory nature of the academy.

Political models stress the centrality of power, influence, and conflict in decision-making processes with respect to change and innovation.

Through the lens of political models, change is viewed as the result of tension between competing ideologies within an organization, with those in power seeking to exert or maintain their influence over those with differing views. In effect, political models suggest that change occurs when the tension between these competing views eventually causes severe discontinuity in an organization, thereby resulting in a rewriting or reframing of power roles. In his *grounded theory of academic change*, Conrad (1978) emphasized the influence of key administrators in bringing about change within colleges and universities. Perhaps not surprisingly, most of the literature on political change models focuses on intrainstitutional change. However, as demonstrated by Parker Palmer's *movement model* (Palmer, 1998), the concepts of power and conflict can be useful with regard to bringing about change at the regional level as well. The movement model suggests that individual initiatives coupled with outreach to those with similar beliefs can spark change both within and beyond organizational boundaries.

Change and innovation in *life-cycle models* is the result of an organization's progression through predetermined stages over the course of time. In general, organizations form, grow, mature, and either reform or die. Life-cycle models, which draw heavily on stage theory and developmental models, are linear and progressive and, while each stage may be shortened or extended based on various internal or external factors, progression through each stage is predetermined. Change efforts in these models are focused on either lengthening the current stage or assisting the organization in progressing from one stage to another. Hence change is viewed at the macro-level and individuals in the organizations are typically viewed simply as players in the structure of the organization.

Social cognition models of change focus on how individuals view organizations and organizational changes through the lenses of sensemaking, construction of knowledge, and cognitive dissonance. In contrast to political models, which focus on differing ideas or values across various groups, social cognition models focus on the conflict of ideas within *individuals*. Change occurs in social cognition models when competing ideas or values collide. This collision forces individuals to reconcile this conflict by changing their behavior, adopting a new idea, or abandoning old values in favor of merged or completely new ones. As this process cascades across members of the organization, individuals' sense of the organization are changed. Social cognition models emphasize the idea that organizational members learn from dissonant thoughts and in turn alter their perceptions in ways that drive organizational learning and change. According to Weick (1995), this sensemaking process usually occurs retroactively; hence change in social cognition models is not linear. Rather, it is interconnected, individual, subjective, and typically internally motivated.

Cultural models focus on the collective beliefs of individuals or groups shaped by the history, values, myths, and rituals of an organization. Perhaps the most ethereal of the six models, cultural change models offer a complex view of bringing about organizational change. Cultural models vary somewhat with regard to their focus on the group or the individual in creating cultural change, but change is typically seen as a long-term process resulting in significant alterations to the organizational mission, values, and norms.

Using Models of Change: Strategic Reflections

Many authors have drawn attention to the unique position of the community college in the educational landscape. As institutions facing the ongoing challenge of change that responds directly to community needs through workforce training, economic development, and transfer programs, community colleges are continuously subject to environmental influences.

In reflecting on the potential efficacy of the six different models, it is important to note that the drivers of change in two-year colleges are many and varied. Depending on the emphases associated with the particular model, the drivers can be categorized as originating within the institution (internal) or from outside of the institution (external). Internal drivers of organizational change include changing academic values, changes in faculty tenure and makeup, and curricular reform. External forces driving change include globalization, market competition, technological changes and developments, resource and funding changes, and legislative action, such as regional coordination mandates or incentives.

Changes in higher education are typically the result of the slow addition and subtraction of functions, programs, and structures. This slow process of change is certainly contrary to the numerous calls for major overhaul and reform of our higher education system from both the public and private sector. While many argue that revolutionary change is necessary, Kezar's (2005) examination of radical changes in academic governance suggests that gradual change is not only a more promising route to lasting change but that radical changes can have many negative consequences for the abilities of institutions to deliver on their missions. The juxtaposition of external pressures for reform coupled with strong organizational biases toward slow incremental change clearly suggests that strong leadership backed by appropriate strategies is necessary to bridge the divide.

Each of the models discussed earlier provides a useful way of illuminating the change process and, when applied in the appropriate circumstance, each has the potential of helping those seeking to advance change to successfully navigate the process. At the same time, each model's assumptions limit its utility. By themselves, none of the models is necessarily a prescription for successful change. But when considered collectively and contextually, these models can help provide practitioners with a framework and accompanying strategies for initiating and implementing change. In two-year colleges, individuals involved in initiating and implementing change should combine their experiences in developing a multi-strategy model of change in order to successfully lead their teams, organizations, or regions through the change process.

A Framework to Guide Change and Innovation in Two-Year Colleges

In proposing a framework, we suggest that viewing change in the context of its source (internal or external) and its locus (institutional or regional) can provide a useful overarching lens through which leaders can in turn choose change strategies most likely to bring about change and innovations. While we acknowledge that many other factors can affect institutional and regional change (such as institutional size, governance, culture, resource availability, and legal issues), we advance this framework as scaffolding on which leaders and their teams can build approaches and strategies to guide their change efforts. In advancing this framework, we extend the discussion of individual models in two major ways. First, our framework suggests that change strategies differ based on the source of the change and the locus of the change. Second, our framework goes beyond organizational-level change and considers changes at the regional level being implemented jointly with other educational institutions, business and industry groups, and governmental agencies.

The framework we present in Figure 9.1 is anchored in our animating proposition that the choice of model(s) for reflecting on change should reflect the *source* (internal or external) and *locus* (institutional or regional) of change. In advancing this model, we invite leaders in and across two-year colleges to reflect on their overall change efforts and in turn select models and accompanying strategies based on their applicability to their particular context. Each quadrant in the model identifies the relevant change models as described in the literature and provides a shorthand notation of the change strategies relevant to the quadrant.

Selecting and Developing Change Strategies

In this final section we identify strategies for bringing about change and innovation in two-year colleges—strategies associated with the source and locus of change—and in turn the various models of change discussed earlier along with examples of these strategies at work in various institutions and regional settings.

Internally Driven Regional Change. We suggest that viewing change through political and social cognitive lenses offers leaders of two-year colleges a nontraditional perspective on the change process, which we have labeled as a *movement*. Movements begin when cognitive dissonance in individuals reaches a point at which one or more persons can no longer tolerate the tension between their values and their organizational reality. Individuals reconcile these differences by changing their behaviors so that

Figure 9.1. An Inclusive Framework

		Source of Change	
		Internal	External
Locus of Change	Regional	**Political** "Start a movement" **Social Cognition** "Speak truth to power"	**Life-Cycle** "Generate, don't stagnate" **Evolutionary** "Responsibly irritate" **Political** "Build a coalition"
	Institution	**Planned Change** "Participative planning" **Social Cognition** "Sensemaking"	**Evolutionary** "Inoculate the organization" **Cultural** "Become a zealot"

they align more closely with their espoused values. By initiating these changes within the context of their organizational reality, they understand that they may risk forgoing myriad benefits of living or working within the organizational structure. Palmer (1998) describes this tipping point as an individual's deciding to no longer live a "divided life." In living undivided lives, individuals accept the consequences of reconciling their behaviors to their ideals even in the face of conflicting organizational practices they may have previously endorsed. Movements are given life when those who have decided to live divided no longer reach out to others with similar beliefs and ideals. Leaders who find themselves with internal conflict regarding the state of their profession or their organization need to reach out to others with similar beliefs. In doing so, they begin to translate private problems into public issues and can activate change.

Meyerson and Scully (1995) describe similar strategies in their work on "tempered radicalism." Given that movements, political change, and the building of understanding through social cognition all require minority and conflicting opinions to stimulate and shape change, among other things, they suggest: (1) experiment to create small wins; (2) take individual authentic actions that challenge the status quo; (3) create and sustain affiliations that develop and maintain multiple perspectives; and (4) maintain fluency in both in-group and out-group languages in order to initiate change.

We suggest that leaders of two-year colleges can adapt these political and social cognition strategies to affect change at the regional level as well. As described earlier, these strategies require that beliefs held within the organization that differ from practices of the established public or regional policy be recognized, surfaced, and then shared with others to promote structural changes. Conrad's (1978) grounded theory of academic change offers clues for how leaders might turn their institutional or inner voices into significant policy reform. In recognizing the discrepancy in power structures, leaders and change agents have the opportunity and the responsibility to respond to the dissonant voices of various interest groups.

Leaders in the movement approach can and should serve as conduits through which organizational views find expression in order to initiate dialogue and plant the seeds of change in the minds of those with the authority to make substantial policy changes. In this way, leaders do not simply scan the environment and respond to perceived external forces. Instead, change is motivated from inside the self or inside the organization with the intent of changing the organizational structures that contribute to the dissonance. Leaders employing these strategies can begin to change power structures through surfacing dissonant ideas and offering options for reform. Through speaking their organization's truth to the regional, legislative, and accrediting powers, leaders challenge those in power to resolve the dissonance at the regional policy level.

An example of the political movement strategy in this quadrant is the Northeast Wisconsin Educational Resource Alliance (NEWERA), which was established in 2000. (A regional case study of NEWERA is presented in Chapter 3.) Leaders in the twelve two-year and four-year colleges located in northeastern Wisconsin recognized the need for regional collaboration to bring about change in order to better serve the education and training needs of the regions' population. What began as an internal dialogue among a few educational leaders has become a regional collaborative partnership spanning more than a decade. NEWERA initiatives have included the establishment of collaborative degree programs, including a Bachelor of Applied Studies (BAS) degree program. Through the participation of the technical colleges and comprehensive four-year colleges, the BAS articulation was the first collaborative degree program in Wisconsin to offer a seamless baccalaureate degree completion between Wisconsin Technical College System colleges and University of Wisconsin institutions. This and other NEWERA projects represent what leaders can do to spark regional change through collaborative movements.

Externally Driven Regional Change. When leaders are charged with adapting their profession and region to changing external circumstances, political strategies associated with the movement model clearly need to be augmented to include evolutionary and life-cycle-based strategies for change as well. We agree with Myran and colleagues (2003) that understanding where an organization is in its life-cycle is a good starting point. Leaders in mature organizations, as well as those at any other stage, can match structure, policies, and practices to the specific stage of the life-cycle. However, the life-cycle theories can be overly self-reflective. When external factors such as legislation, resource depletion, enrollment fluctuations, and regional economic cycles force changes, strategies focused on improving accountability, demonstrating value, and being fiscally responsible may serve to turn the lens too far inward, leaving our organizations self-absorbed. While these metrics may be necessary or even mandated for survival, we believe that leaders should take the opportunity to be "generative," focusing and refocusing the efforts of their institutions and profession on those whom we serve and, in doing so, craft educational experiences that are responsive to regional needs.

Evolutionary strategies provide yet another opportunity for leaders. Stagnation in evolutionary terms means death. Leaders of two-year colleges need to realize that maintaining the equilibrium in an organization is not a change strategy and, in evolutionary terms, those who do not use external cues as a way to initiate change will die. Rather than decrying the continual pressure and simply attempting to mitigate the external in favor of maintaining the status quo, leaders at every level should seek to intentionally disturb the status quo, responsibly irritate systems, and challenge systems to reorganize to meet the demands of the new environment.

Leaders who take seriously the charge of being generative and a "responsible irritant" can be successful only through building coalitions. Using the political insights of the movement model, leaders must seek to build coalitions of individuals and organizations that share their viewpoint and coalesce the ideas that exist regionally into a power base that can effectively challenge the status quo. They must balance both sides of the responsible-irritant equation very carefully. Successful application of this principle requires that leaders understand the regional tolerance for and political will to change. After all, too much irritation, like an asteroid striking the earth, leaves little time for adaptation and, like the dinosaurs, our institutions may become extinct.

Generative leaders recognize that individual institutions may not always be able to serve the needs of their regions, and in turn many consortia exhibit the qualities of regional change through coalition building. The Midwest Community College Health Information Technology Consortium (MWHIT) is one example of the generative strategies that two-year college leaders can use to effect regional change. Through the partnership of seventeen community colleges across ten Midwestern states, the consortium's goal to educate 2,700 health informatics workers in six disciplines is designed to address the need for nearly 50,000 health-related information technology workers in the next five years. Such ambitious, but clearly necessary, training efforts require broad regional collaboration, and the MWHIT consortium can serve as a model for how to translate the external source of change (labor market needs) into regional changes that meet the needs of Midwestern states.

Internally Driven Institutional Change.   Planned change strategies dominate the literature on organizational change, and these strategies have a place in the tool box of change agents when put in the context of the unique nature of higher education. While they are not a panacea for every circumstance and every situation, planned change models in two-year colleges can be usefully applied in situations where the source of change is internal and the locus of change is institutional. Mintzberg (1994) suggests a basic five-step planned change strategy: (1) set college objectives; (2) complete an external analysis; (3) identify internal issues and opportunities; (4) evaluate potential strategies, and (5) operationalize objectives through resource allocation. We suggest that in the context of planned change, where positional power allows for legitimate authority, leaders must temper traditional central planning and top-down principles with strategies that allow individuals and groups within the college to both form and be formed by the planning process. Building in feedback loops with stakeholders and making those feedback loops a formal part of the change process is critical to effective planned change on campus. Such actions coupled with targeted communication strategies like community forums, open campus dialogues, and regular written communications can serve to increase campus buy-in and bring to the surface any conflicting ideas before the implementation stage of a planned-change process. An examination by Eddy (2003) of planned-change efforts at five two-year campuses supports this notion. She found that planned-change processes can produce tangible results for colleges but that the examined planned changes frequently failed to generate broad-based and lasting actions when communication was infrequent, disjointed, or limited to a small number of campus insiders.

One function of frequent, accurate, and open communication in the change process is that of *sensemaking*. Karl Weick (1995) suggests strategies that assist individuals within organizations in making sense of change efforts. Leaders who help those within their organizations construct and interpret change efforts are more likely to align efforts and realize change within their organizations. They must first understand the cues that those in their organizations are using to construct their individual realities and then assist in stretching individual and organizational understanding by offering ongoing plausible alternative explanations. Understanding that sensemaking occurs retroactively is also very important to leading successful change. In doing so, we are reminded that good upfront communication about change processes must be reinforced by good sensemaking dialogues throughout.

NEW DIRECTIONS FOR COMMUNITY COLLEGES • DOI: 10.1002/cc

The Academic Quality Improvement Program (AQIP) sponsored by the Higher Learning Commission is an example of the evolution of institutional planning in higher education. AQIP encompasses both the planned change approach suggested by Mintzberg and the sensemaking through collaborative and open communication strategy discussed by Weick. The Higher Learning Commission uses AQIP as an alternative accreditation process for institutions focused on using the tools of quality and continuous improvement to advance institutional objectives. The nine AQIP categories, which span operations, communications, student learning, and institutional relationships provide a framework for leaders at all levels of two-year colleges to involve multiple stakeholder groups in planning institutional-level changes.

Nearly four hundred institutions across the Midwest have now adopted the AQIP planning process to meet institutional goals and share successes across the higher education community. The successes and challenges of internal planning for institutional-level change are shared among member colleges and are available to other interested members of the higher education community in the "Action Project Directory" section of the AQIP Web site (http://www.ncahlc.org/aqip-home/). Leaders might consider implementing the strategies used by AQIP-member community colleges to drive innovation and change.

Externally Driven Institutional Change.   As earlier discussed, two-year colleges are repeatedly portrayed as highly and uniquely responsive to environmental forces. In this context, Baker (1998) proposed the *core values model*, in which leaders, driven by external forces, adapt systems and processes to affect individual and institutional outcomes. When external factors challenge the mission, culture, and systems of a college, the evolutionary response of the organization is typically protectionist. In countering this response, leaders need to consider strategies similar to the immunization process. Determining how and what information can breach the organization's protective barrier is the first step. In this way, leaders are the hypodermic needle delivering the medicine to the veins of the organization. As leaders inoculate the organization, they can anticipate their efforts at introducing the change to be met by a strong "immune response" from certain pockets of the organization. Leaders can use many strategies to combat this resistance. Changing policy, structure, and reward systems can suppress the organization's response to the change long enough for the organization to adapt appropriately to the new environment.

While the adaptive framework provides some guidance for leaders seeking to institute organizational change, close attention must also be paid to the organizational culture. An understanding from leaders that cultures are built around organizational and regional visions, values, rituals, ceremonies, histories, and symbols is critical. Through the continuous process of delivering targeted doses of information coupled with changes to existing structures, leaders can go a long way toward changing the culture of the college.

In order for campus leaders to have an impact on culture, they must consider becoming zealots for their institutions and those whom they serve. True believers in the cause who understand the organizational history and can glimpse the future can impact organizational culture through a number of strategies.

Deal and Peterson (1999) suggest three broad strategies for changing school cultures: pioneering, overhauling, and evolving. Whether beginning something new, changing a broken system, or making adjustments to a culture, leaders should pay close attention to the factors that contribute to culture. In order to effectively change cultures leaders should possess and develop a compelling shared vision for the future. Similar to the planned-change strategies discussed earlier, this vision absolutely must be done collaboratively and authentically. Establishing the urgency of change and keeping the organization appropriately stretched between what *is* and what *can be* is critical in changing culture. Once a shared vision has been established, careful tending and reinforcement are clearly necessary to continue any cultural shift. As zealots, leaders model the core assumptions and beliefs of the college and also serve as the chief storyteller. Through symbol, ritual, ceremony, habit, and dialogue leaders facilitate organizational learning and growth. By reinforcing the cultural practices consistent with the vision and discouraging or eliminating practices that are not, leaders can align individuals and groups in advancing change and innovation.

One way in which leaders of two-year colleges can inoculate their organizations is through obtaining and measuring feedback from the communities they serve. Delta College, which serves the central part of Michigan, has expanded its internal planning process through comprehensive and inclusive dialogue with key stakeholders and surveying of local employers and other constituents in an effort to bring external perspectives to the institutional change process.

We believe that such outreach efforts are often critical to the success of internal change efforts and that it is the role of leaders to bring external perspective to their campuses. To wit, Delta's efforts have resulted in the identification of more than ninety unmet needs by its stakeholders. If our institutions are to continue to advance, we must be willing and prepared as leaders to utilize multiple methods for inviting realities external to our organizations.

Conclusion

In order for leaders of two-year colleges in the Midwest to successfully lead our colleges in driving the future of the nation, we must not only embrace the concept of change but be armed with strategies that can assist those in our departments, colleges, communities, and regions to act on their visions of change and innovation. In order to effect these changes leaders should:

NEW DIRECTIONS FOR COMMUNITY COLLEGES • DOI: 10.1002/cc

- Understand the source and the locus of the change as a critical first step in determining which strategies will be most effective for advancing regional partnerships with appropriate institutional support.
- Employ political and movement models to translate private organizational challenges into public issues. Through outreach and dialogue to other similar organizations, the silent internal problems can find voice and spur change.
- Ensure the frequency and quality of interaction between stakeholders and college faculty and staff, recognizing that internal changes can be expedited and enhanced from external pressures. Effectively engaging external partners will help the college recognize the need for change and will result in less drastic organizational shifts.

It is our hope that the framework, models, and strategies discussed herein contribute to the ongoing dialogue regarding change and innovation within and across our two-year colleges in the Midwest. We are confident that these institutions can effectively rise to the challenge and continue to effectively serve our communities and our nation.

Looking beyond the Midwest, the expansion of regional alliances requires community college leaders to think and act differently when introducing change. As we have argued, the preferred strategies for supporting external, regionally focused change (i.e., political coalition building, generative change) are particularly responsive to the drivers and challenges of regional economic recovery (e.g., linking applied research and technology transfer practices, building rural human resource development capacity).

References

Baker, George A., III. *Managing Change: A Model for Community College Leaders.* Washington, D.C.: Community College Press, 1998.

Conrad, C. F. "A Grounded Theory of Academic Change." *Sociology of Education,* 1978, *51,* 101–112.

Deal, T. E., and Peterson, K. D. *Shaping School Culture: The Heart of Leadership.* San Francisco: Jossey-Bass, 1999.

Eddy, P. L. "Sensemaking on Campus: How Community College Presidents Frame Change." *Community College Journal of Research & Practice,* 2003, 27(6), 453.

Goodman, P. S. *Change in Organizations: New Perspectives on Theory, Research, and Practice.* San Francisco: Jossey-Bass, 1982.

Kezar, A. "Theories and Models of Organizational Change." *ASHE-ERIC Higher Education Report,* 2001, 28(4), 25–59.

Kezar, A. "Consequences of Radical Change in Governance: A Grounded Theory Approach." *Journal of Higher Education,* 2005, 76(6), 634–668.

Kezar, A., and Eckel, P. D. "The Effect of Institutional Culture on Change Strategies in Higher Education." *Journal of Higher Education,* 2002, 73(4), 435–460.

Meyer, A. D., Brooks, G. R., and Goes, J. B. "Environmental Jolts and Industry Revolutions: Organizational Responses to Discontinuous Change." *Strategic Management Journal,* 1990, *11,* 93–110.

Meyerson, D. E., and Scully, M. A. "Tempered Radicalism and the Politics of Ambivalence and Change." *Organization Science*, 1995, 6(5), 585–600.

Mintzberg, H. *The Rise and Fall of Strategic Planning.* New York: The Free Press, 1994.

Myran, G., Baker, G. A., III, Simone, B., and Zeiss, T. *Leadership Strategies for Community College Executives.* Washington, D.C.: Community College Press, 2003.

Palmer, P. J. *The Courage to Teach: Exploring the Inner Landscape of a Teacher's Life.* San Francisco: Jossey-Bass, 1998.

Weick, K. E. *Sensemaking in Organizations.* Thousand Oaks: Sage Publications, 1995.

CHRISTOPHER J. MATHENY *is vice president and chief academic officer at Fox Valley Technical College in Appleton, Wisconsin.*

CLIFTON CONRAD *is a professor of Higher Education in the Department of Educational Leadership and Policy Analysis at the University of Wisconsin–Madison.*

NEW DIRECTIONS FOR COMMUNITY COLLEGES • DOI: 10.1002/cc

INDEX

Academic Quality Improvement Program (AQIP; Higher Learning Commission), 121; database (Worldwide Instructional Design Systems), 91, 92

Achieving the Dream (ATD): Community Colleges Count network, 11

Adult basic education (ABE), 54, 56, 60, 62, 63, 65

Adult Education and Family Literacy Act (Workforce Investment Act), 55

Advancing the Regional Role of Two-Year Colleges in the Twenty-First Century (New Directions for Community Colleges), 84

Affolter-Caine, B., 18, 54

Akon-Ramsey Community College (Minnesota), 103

Alcohol and Other Drug Abuse (AODA) associate degree (College of Menominee Nation), 33

Alfonso, M., 109

American Association of Universities, 98

American Chemical Society, 103

American Diploma Project, 72

American Graduation Initiative (AGI), 10

American Midwest, 17

America's Recovery and Reinvestment Act (ARRA), 25

Ann Arbor, Michigan, 22–23

Antigo, Wisconsin, 49–50

Appleton, Wisconsin, 36

Association of American Colleges and Universities (AAC&U), 86–87

Atkinson, R., 67

Austin, J., 2–3, 12, 17, 18, 54, 101

Auto-Region community college consortium, 26

Bailey, T., 94, 109

Baker, G. A., III, 111, 119, 121

Barr, R. B., 88

Bay Lake Commission (Wisconsin), 36

Bloomington, Indiana, 22–23

Boston University, 104, 105

Bragg, D. D., 3, 12, 13, 53, 64, 83–84, 86, 87

Bransford, J. D., 83–84, 88

Brint, S. G., 84, 86

Brookings Institute, 2–3, 18

Brookings Metropolitan Policy Program, 101

Brooks, G. R., 113

Brown, A. L., 83–84, 88

Brown, J. S., 69

Canada, 18

Career and Technical Education (CTE), Carl D. Perkins IV legislation on, 59

Carnegie Mellon University, 23

Case Western Reserve, 23

Caught in the Middle: America's Heartland in the Age of Globalism (Longworth), 8, 18

Center for American Progress, 88

Center for the Study of Community Colleges (CSCC), 85, 86

Center on Wisconsin Strategy, 59

Change (journal), 88

Chesbrough, H., 67–69

Chicago, Illinois, 9, 103

Chicago Council on Global Affairs, 18

Chicagoland Chamber of Commerce, 70–71

Chippewa Valley Technical College (Wisconsin) Health Education Center, 48–49

Christensen, C., 75

City Colleges of Chicago, 55

Cleveland, Ohio, 9, 18, 23

Cleveland, Wisconsin, 49

Coakley, C. A., 8

Cocking, R. R., 83–84, 88

Cohen, A. M., 85, 86

College of Menominee Nation (Wisconsin), 30, 33

Common Core Standards, 24

Community college, and research university collaboration: and changing research and innovation context, 98–100; implications of, for practice, 109; leverage challenges for, 108–109; new roles for, 100–103; and relationships between selected high-impact activities and clusters of effective

125